CW00552016

All the mistakes...

... you could make or avoid when starting a business in Ireland

by

Peter Cronin

ardú Press

A CIP catalogue record for this book is available from the British Library.
ISBN 978-1-905597-93-2

Printed in UK.
The papers used in this book were produced in an environmentally friendly way from sustainable forests.

Dedicated to the memory of my father, Geoffrey Cronin who taught me, by example, how to mentor.

ardú Press
Unit 2, Idea House, Killarney Road, Bray, Co. Wicklow, Ireland

Contents

Author's Foreword

I started my first business at the age of 14 repairing the bicycles of the neighbourhood children. It was definitely an indication of the future, though I never recognised that at the time.

I remember being told at an interview at the age of 17 that I had a lot of confidence for someone so young and inexperienced. The interviewer was right, but so was I.

I realised, when I was made redundant on my 21st birthday that I wasn't really cut out to be an employee. I haven't really had a job since then. I have always worked for myself.

Most of the learnings in this book are self-taught by doing all the wrong things before doing the right things. There is one thing that I hope you learn from this book.

It's cheaper to learn from the mistakes of others than it is to learn by making the mistakes yourself!

While this is not a workbook, and not every person who reads it will start a business, I've identified a strategy that is transferrable across businesses and markets that makes the whole process easier. It is not in a perfect order either but it fits the concept of *Ready, Aim, Fire* as you launch your business. It is written in an Irish context so the tax and support structures are Irish focused. We are, after all, a great country in which to do business.

I wish you luck on your entrepreneurial journey and I hope I can save you from making at least a few of the mistakes that I have made.

I would love your feedback via *www.ardu.ie*

Or: *@business_dr* on twitter
Or: *https://www.linkedin.com/in/businessdr* on LinkedIn
Or: just call my office *+ 353 1 284 1105*

Part One

Ready

Ready

To be ready to start a business is one thing. For it to be the right time to do it can be quite another. That's why I've broken down the early stage of the process into five parts and this is the longest section of the book.

I learned that when you are not sure where to start you should do two things:

1. Sweep the floor.
   This has two impacts:

   a) Anyone working with you sees that you are happy to get 'down and dirty'
   b) You clear your mind by doing something simple and practical that, although it needs little thought, requires a good degree of attention to detail

2. Sharpen the tools.
   If you are a carpenter this is obvious: sharp tools get through work easier than blunt ones. Why shouldn't that be true of the tools of your business?

The biggest and most valuable tool you can have in operating a business is knowledge.

So our first key word is: **RESEARCH**

As you look into starting a business that makes you [according to Enterprise Ireland (EI)] a *latent* entrepreneur. Latent is described as *Embryonic* or *Underdeveloped* and without research that is what you are. We will break the research down into bite-sized pieces of information that you need to gather in order to make the right kind of informed decision.

The second key word is: **EDUCATE**

What do you already know? Honestly, what do you need to learn if you are to make as few mistakes as possible? The difficulty with this is how are you supposed to know what it is that you don't know? You don't know it, but you get what I mean.

The next word is: **APPLY**

Ireland is a great country in which to do business; or so former Taoiseach Enda Kenny told us many times. The level of financial and other supports available to first time entrepreneurs is huge. I think you would be crazy to start a business without first **APPLY**ING for some of these supports.

The next word is: **DRIVE**

Having educated yourself, the hardest part of starting a business is to prevent yourself from getting sucked into spending your entire time on operations. A business without a strategy is really just a job with a series of different employers. *You*, the business owner, have to **DRIVE** the business.

And the final 'word' is: *YEAR 1 Business Plan*

You are not ready to start a business without a plan. That plan is a roadmap to a destination. It is up to *you* to decide where that destination is. In what units will you measure the success of the first year in business? If you are driving the business wouldn't it help to know the destination of the journey?

At the end of each chapter you will find a checklist. See how many boxes you can tick before you start to read. Then try again when you think you are READY.

Chapter 1:
Research

I am breaking this into bite sized pieces because there is so much you need to know before you start. The main things you need to know about are:

A. Myself: – Look in the Mirror
B. The Customers.
   What do they need?
   What do they want?
C. The competitors.
   How do *they* currently meet the Customer's needs
D. The opportunity

A. Look in the Mirror

In our Entrepreneurial life we always have goals and I will talk about those later. But if we are to be successful in business there are a number of points or milestones that are significant in our development as business people.

Often you will hear people discuss whether the entrepreneur is born or made.

So as you set out on a journey towards entrepreneurship, I suggest a good long look in the mirror to ask yourself:

Is this the right decision at the right time for ME?

There are a great many things that need to fall into place if the answer to that question is to be yes.

They include (but are not limited to):

- Attitude
- Business Skills / Training
- Competitor Knowledge
- Customer Profiling
- Family support
- Finance
- IT issues
- Marketability
- Marketing Strategy
- Planning
- You, and what happens in your head

The list is obviously in alphabetical order and equally the list is incomplete. I just want to focus on *You* and your *Attitude*.

When I work with a new client I like to know as much as I can about the journey they have been on to bring them to today. That usually means me asking 'why' questions.

- Why did you make this choice or that at this point?
- Why was that the right choice at that time?
- Why are you choosing to be self-employed anyway?
  Would you not do, like your parents always wanted, and get yourself a permanent and pensionable job?

- Why NOT?
  I am assuming *not,* because you are reading this
- What were the significant moments or decisions that led you down the road that eventually brought you to the decision?

What I am trying to reach towards is: What motivates the entrepreneur? Is it *towards* motivation: This is such a great idea, I always wanted to do this… or *away* motivation: I don't want to be a wage slave like such and such or I don't want someone who knows less than I do telling me how to do it. If you know whether you are towards or away motivated then you are half way there.

What about the key influencers in your life?

Usually, with entrepreneurs, it boils down to some combination of just three key influences:

1. A Role Model (Nurture)
   indicating that entrepreneurs are made not born
2. The number of ideas you've had every day, ever since you were a child, led to the inescapable reality that the only real option was self-employment (Nature) indicating that entrepreneurs are born not made
3. And increasingly in the past 10 years the solid awareness that, while there *is* indeed work out there, quite often there are not jobs but gigs available. And this creates what I call the reluctant entrepreneur

I've recognised along the journey that there is almost always a key influencer. There is almost always a role model: a teacher who encourages a teenager, the financially supportive relative, the mentor, the older person who listens. Almost every entrepreneur can identify one or more of these in their lives.

These amazing mentors together contribute to the development of the entrepreneur. As you start on the journey think: Who are my influencers? and then go and talk to them.

Fifteen percent of the CAO (*University Central Applications Office*) applications in 2018 sought a business degree and according to an Enterprise Ireland survey 57% of people planning to start a business have a degree while only 20% have a leaving cert or similar (apprenticeship or Level 5 QQI). Does that mean an entrepreneur needs a degree to succeed? You decide.

So what forms an entrepreneur? (This is the bit where I prove my 'opinionated' title).

In my opinion, the entrepreneur is influenced by many different factors, in varying degrees, and is often tipped over into business by one of them. But there is no single magic ingredient. I have, however, noticed that all the entrepreneurs I have met share three characteristics in varying degrees; so, in no particular order.

1. A positive attitude to risk
2. An endless supply of emotional resilience
3. A view of the world that varies from the norm in some way

So, when the notion of starting a business comes to mind and you look in the mirror the first time, ask yourself:

What is my attitude to life, risk and how do I respond to adversity?

Then decide on what influences have come to bear to bring you to the verge of this decision.

If you are happy with your truthful responses to these questions there are just four last questions.

1. Does my idea have the legs to financially support me? if yes, it's a business, if not it's a hobby
2. Do I have the requisite skills? If not can I buy them in at a rate that works?
3. What alternatives to this idea have I considered?
4. Do I have the support of my loved ones?

If you are satisfied with your responses to all of this then you might just be an entrepreneur.

There are hundreds of personality profile products on the market. As you start a business you need to have maximum information about yourself. Don't be shy about gaining self-awareness. Take one or even two of these tests.

I am not recommending any specific test. But here are a few that it might help you to try. They are freely available on the web.

1. Myers Briggs type Indicator
2. The Enneagram
3. Disc Profile or ABCD personality types

There are also tests for Leadership, Creativity and such things as Emotional IQ. Knowing your personal strengths and weaknesses empowers you to move on beyond where you are today.

B. Who is my Customer?

I'll start this section with a question. If you don't know where you are going how will you get there? You are reaching out to a customer. They are the first stop on the journey. What makes most businesses vulnerable is that they have no idea who their customer is or, in the more extreme cases, if there is a customer at all. They just take the money from whoever comes through the door without really trying to connect with the customer. Surely we want to move that customer from a one-time shopper through to a repeat customer and on to a raving fan of the business.

I believe that what every business needs is a cohort of raving fans talking (positively) about your business to their friends. In essence they are living, believable advertisements. Of course we are happy to take what comes through the door. But that's not enough if we are to market successfully. The small business has to be much more precise than the large one because it can't just throw money at the problem.

Getting the process of converting interest into sales is the real skill. Michael Smurfit always maintained that it is easier (and cheaper) to sell more product to an existing customer than it is to go out and prospect for a new one. So, once the customer has bought from you once, what does it take to generate sale number two? The next stage is getting them to repeat repeatedly. Then finally you want them to refer you on. What most businesses do is to advertise *looking* for a customer instead of *identifying and pursuing* the desired customer or group of customers.

It seems to me that most of the time, when you start the process, the business owner says "*I have all kinds of customers".* That's a perception but not a fact. What the truth usually is – and I've seen it time after time – We have lots of tyre kickers who do not spend any money and then we have the customers who actually buy something.

When we look at who spends the money, we find usually that 80% of the money is coming from a small group of customers who fit a specific profile. On that basis, we want to attract the maximum number *of the right type of customers.* Different businesses have different targets and indeed I need to break this down to Business-to-Consumer (B2C) and Business-to-Business (B2B).

In B2C We can test by gender, age, socio-economic classification, geography and so on.

Case Study 1 – B2C
A beautician working in Dublin 17.

> She starts by thinking her customers are *all women* from 17 to 70 (***Mistake!***) but quickly recognises that 80% of her clients are 25–35 in age. When she looks a bit deeper she finds that most of them are employed in clerical roles in Dublin city centre. Now she has them geographically, by age, by gender and by spending power. She can pitch her price to suit an amount that they can afford to spend, weekly or monthly.

> Knowledge is power. It also means that she can write her marketing material to speak specifically to her target. After all what attracts a 25–35 year old is very different from the message you send to a 55+ customer. We can discuss this more when we are on the marketing topic.

B2B can be more difficult.

Case Study 2 – B2B

A computer technician based in Waterford:

He has a B2C business fixing broken computers for households but the work is not consistent enough to make the business secure. He decides to move towards the commercial sector (B2B) in the hope of more repeat work from fewer customers.

So he decides to look for work among the small-business community. He has to decide whose business he wants? First question is what size of business? He recognises that the one man show is very similar to his B2C customer and will only call when something is broken. He can't handle the big companies so, by default, he targets businesses with more than two and less than ten employees. Now he needs to ask what industry sector? Retail? That requires specific point of sale software knowledge so not really the best option for the quick fix he needs. What he identifies is that there are lots of small offices with networks and servers so he decided to target them. He quickly also notices that those offices are either in service industry or are B2B themselves.

Next he has to look at geography. A 10km radius of base means he won't spend all day travelling and not getting paid for that time. If 10km is not generating enough he can widen it in 5km increments and include additional targets until he reaches the right number of repeating clients. If someone finds him on the internet that's a bonus but his *target* customer, the customer whose business he has specifically chosen to pursue, is identified and targeted by doing some research. Now he can tailor his marketing material specifically to his desired customer.

If it is possible to identify the target customer by name then you have a much higher than average chance of getting the sale. Simply, if you know about the person it is much easier to tailor the message so that they are more receptive to your pitch.

This means too that, once captured, you need to foster a relationship with your customer in order to achieve phases 2 and 3 of the process. To cement phase one and *acquire the customer* put yourself in their shoes. What is it that would make you buy from a business a second time? This is where you can spend really valuable time getting inside the customer's head.

Ask yourself the following question:

What would make your relationship with the customer invaluable, so that you become their provider of choice?

Finally, when getting to know your customer, it is very important to get to know their *point of pain* and see how *you* can be the paracetamol for that headache.

C. The Competition

Time after time, when I ask about their competition, entrepreneurs assert that they do not have any.

This is based on the assumption that if someone does not provide *exactly* the same service or product that they do then they are not a competitor. (**Mistake!**) When you see it written down like this you know what utter rubbish that statement is.

Every business that wants the customer to spend the same money as you want, is your competitor.

So what research should you do?
Get on the internet and look for competitors. Ask any 20 people what they would put into a search engine (Google, Bing, Wiki and so on) in order to find a business like yours. Once you find out what they would put into a search engine, do it and see who comes up in the search results. Now you know who your first line competitors are.

Next, visit the competitor's website. Identify what they do that most closely resembles your offering or targets the same customer. Go into their business or get on the phone and play customer. Put yourself in the client's shoes and find the things you like and the things you don't about your competitors business. It doesn't matter whether it is the customer service, the product, some piece of after sales, an upsell or the way they relate to you as a customer. Just identify where they are strong and where they both meet, and fail to meet, the customer expectations. You could also do an old fashioned "mystery shop" attempting to return a product and test *that* weakness.

Once you have made this assessment of four or five competitors, you are going to spot trends. Those trends might be opportunities for you. Whether it is just in copying good practice (learning from the competitor's mistakes) or filling glaring holes in the competitor's customer offering, doesn't matter. This research will prevent you from making rookie mistakes, so don't skip it. If you want to take it to its logical conclusion, do a **SWOT** analysis (**S**trengths, **W**eaknesses, **O**pportunities and **T**hreats) of the competitor and then look and see if you can duplicate the strengths and exploit the weaknesses to grow your customer base.

Opportunity – an example: Back in 2003 Apple invested heavily when looking for a new font to promote their products. Lots of money was spent on market research to identify the perfect font. Remember that Apple and Adobe (who designed the font) are market leaders in the graphic design world. Now, while I don't know the details of *why* this is the best font, I do know that they will have done everything they could get the right font. They've used it for 16 years. So we have used the same font for this book because of Apple's very expensive market research. Sometimes it pays off to just copy the big guys.

Price:
Competitor research also gives you a strong indication about what you should charge for your service or product. A larger competitor will already have figured out what the market will carry and will be charging it. I never encourage start-ups to compete on price but on the other hand it might be a part of the package that gives you the edge.

The final place that competitor research helps you is in defining your position in the market. Your position in the market is relative to all the other players. Perhaps you have a more complete offering, or you have a specific target audience, or you have a unique twist on your offering. The price you charge should reflect the ability of the target customer to pay. Do you want to be perceived as a 'low-price high-volume' offering? Or are you a 'premium product' only looking for a premium audience at a premium or exclusive price? What impact would that decision have on the value of sales?

The Deluxe option

The word exclusive is really interesting. It implies that your product is better because some customers are excluded from owning or using it on grounds of the price. It similarly implies that the client can only buy it from you. Does that therefore mean that you should be charging more because, if they want it, they have no choice but to buy it from you?

One example of this is the expensive sports car which only the very wealthy can afford to buy, own and run. Does Ferrari show their cars on the same street as the Fiat showrooms, even though they are in fact the same company? No, they do not, because they address different markets. Nevertheless they *do* co-operate in the research and development stage.

Which of your competitors would you choose co-operate with? Or could there be an opportunity for you to sub-contract to them?

D. The Opportunity

Many people starting a business do so because they have spotted what they perceive to be 'a gap in the market'. This makes you either very smart, first in the market or not smart at all.

If you are very smart then you have spotted a demand that is as yet unmet or is at least poorly or inadequately met.

The question I ask is:

**If there is a gap in the market
is there a market in the gap?**

Is there actually a demand for what you propose? Before you spend any money you need to find out what Joe Public thinks. We will discuss the *Hows* of that in the Market Research section. Suffice to say at this stage that you need to be very sure that there is a reasonable chance that the revenue from this gap will be sufficient, in a year or two, to fully replace your current source of income. The Business from this gap has to pay its own way and provide you with a stable income.

Lots of people come up with an idea for something they could make and then they go out and try to sell it to a *not very clearly defined* target customer. (**Mistake!**) The smarter option, in my view, comes from my own business mentor. He said it in one simple phrase.

*Don't try to sell what you can make
find something you can sell, and make that.*

In line with this, you also need to assess the cost (the *real* cost) of setting up. There are a lot of costs that many people forget to budget for, so I include a list of possible set-up costs. You might need some, or all, of the things included on it. I am not suggesting it is exhaustive. You may already have many of these sorted out but they constitute your investment in your business so you should put a value on that investment.

Can you find the money to pay for the set up cost?
Where will you get the money to do so if not? If you have to borrow, how much will it cost to repay per month? Indeed, will you have to write a business plan for a financial institution in order to secure funding? These are all considerations BEFORE you go any further. Ignoring this is another *mistake*.

Here are two lists. In the first list they are all **one-off costs**. In the second list they are repeating costs but you may have to pay the total cost for the first year at the beginning. The lists are alphabetic rather than in any order of priority.

- Broadband
- Business phone
- Company formation
- Compliance costs (Safety statement, method statements, Safepass, Driver CPC, First Aid, Manual Handling, Fire Safety, Other Training courses etc.)
- Computer
- CRO and similar registrations
- First aid kit (for the office or vehicle)
- Franchise fees or licencing for the right to sell your product
- Furniture

- Fire extinguishers
  (advisable even if working at home)
- IT networks
- Legal fees
- Logo/ Brand design & Business cards etc.
- Patent or trademark
- Premises fit-out
- Printer
- Promotional materials
- Specialist software
- Tools & Equipment
- Vehicle & any fit-out it might need
- Website & Search Engine Optimisation

First time costs with possible up-front payments:
- Insurances
  - Public Liability / Product Liability / Professional Indemnity
  - Business-use motor insurance
- Licences for software (e.g. Microsoft, Accounts package, CRM software)
- Membership of professional bodies
- Mandatory registrations (RECI, PSAI, RIAI)
- Utility installation (phones, broadband, electricity, waste disposal, etc.)

I believe that very often, for almost every entrepreneur there is work out there as a sub-contractor to one of your larger competitors. That work will stabilise the income stream, and gain you market credibility, as you start the business. It can be done alongside developing your customer base. Where is that opportunity for you? Just one more bit of research.

The final thing to check whether you have any Intellectual Property that you might be wise to protect with a patent or a trademark. This is a specialist area, not for a book like this as I could not do it any kind of justice. Nevertheless you should discuss it with the Patents Office if you think you have something to protect. They are the relevant experts. If there is something patentable then your entire business model might change to one of licencing someone to produce the product, and you get a fee for every one sold. That would give you passive income. Money for not working: I like that idea.

Checklist of Research Tasks

ACTION	☑
Look in the mirror	☐
Write down in 50 words or less WHY you want to do this	☐
Do a personal SWOT analysis	☐
Decide how you will address the weaknesses and threats	☐
Deliver on that decision	☐
Do a personal budget using the mabs budget tool *https://www.mabs.ie/en/how_we_help/debt_and_budgeting_tools/mabs_budgeting.html*	☐
Talk to your family and ensure they are in FULL support	☐
Do the preliminary customer research – Not with family or friends, they will often just tell you what they think you want to hear	☐
Calculate the set-up costs	☐
Target a source for the set-up funding	☐
Find out what regulation applies to your industry	☐
Read the rest of this book and complete the checklists	☐

Chapter 2:
Educate

The one assumption that I am making is that you have the core skill to deliver the product or service and that you don't have to learn to do it in the first place.

The entire thrust of your research phase is a knowledge gathering exercise. Knowledge gives you power. You recognise that you have made a lot of assumptions and discovered that there are many things that you don't know about the business. That power gives you a strategic and management advantage over your competitors because they probably don't have that knowledge about themselves.

Any time you start a project you need to clear the desk and at least figuratively start with a clean sheet of paper. I suggest three pages.

A. What Do you Know?
Page 1:
List ALL the skills that you bring to the business. Every competence that might be required should be included. Whether it's sweeping the floor or research and decision making and, of course, including your ability to deliver the core work of the business. As a sub list you might list any qualifications you have that might lend credibility to

your new business. The length of the list should be well into the 20s.

B. What do you need to learn?
Page 2:
List as many of the things you have discovered that you don't have enough expertise in as possible. Once you have written the list it leads to yet more questions that you have to answer for yourself.

- What things will I learn to do myself?
- What will it be more efficient to buy in?
- Which will be better use of my time and money?

Often at this point in the project you have more time than money and that tends to make the immediate decision for you. However while it is really important that in the beginning you can do every job in the business at least competently if not brilliantly, you should have a longer view. Over time what will be the first tasks you delegate or automate?

If you intend to grow the business beyond a turnover that pays just you a living wage you need to put a plan in place for some kind of customer relationship management system. That system should probably be linked to your invoicing and accounts systems. While you won't need all the functionality of a system like that at the start of your business, you won't have time to put it in place at the point where you need it. So I suggest doing it at the start.

Everyone starting a business should do a Start your own Business course. Yes you might already know some of the content but there are three good reasons to do the training.

1. Tutor expertise.
2. Other Learner expertise and experience
3. The opportunity to network with other start-ups

If you like to look at it differently there is an opportunity to learn formally and also informally. The uncertified learning, driven by your desire to know, is most important. It is your need to educate yourself about the things you discovered that you *didn't* know, through the research phase, that can be the difference between the success and the failure of the business.

So what should you ensure that you have learned about in advance of actually pushing the button on your business?

Let's do the list alphabetically. This time I am suggesting why you should be sure to educate yourself on this. *Ignoring this is a fatal mistake*.

I will provide basic information on most of the topics throughout the book but since there is at least a chapter in each of the headings below there are things I just can't fit into this book.

Accounts
You have to understand what the accounts tell you and the best way to understand is to put the data in yourself, at least at the beginning.

Compliance
You have certain legal requirements to comply with. Safety statement, perhaps Safepass or Driver cpc, you might have to be on a register like the Private Security Authority or the

Sustainable Energy Authority of Ireland, and you definitely have to register for tax and will need tax clearance.

Employment
If you decide to have employees (or even sub-contractors in some cases) you will have to recruit, interview and assess performance. You will be governed by a lot of legislation. Contracts are required. You need an employee handbook. There are implications whether the person is full-time, part-time, casual or sub-contractor – there is a whole chapter on this (Chapter 10).

Finance
I will deal with this in detail later. Before you read the finance section make sure you have completed the first checklist on page 25.

Insurance
If you deal with customers whether B2B or B2C some time there will be an incident, accident or mistake. At that point you want the protection of an insurer. You might also want to consider keyman insurance. You will have to have appropriate motor cover.

Market Research
I have already addressed this area in the Research Section. It has to be complete before you move on.

Marketing
Unless people are aware that your business, and its offering, there will not be any customers. Marketing is the communication of a specific message to targeted businesses or individuals with the express intention of encouraging them to buy. This you have to master. I will address it in much greater depth later.

Management

Someone has to literally keep an eye on all the aspects of the business all the time. It is always the one you take your eye off that goes wrong (Murphy's Law I suppose). While I will address this in more detail later; there are two nuggets worth considering at this stage.

1. Test and measure every action so that you know what result it is likely to deliver

2. If it cannot be measured it cannot be managed

Pay Related Social Insurance (PRSI)

You need to pay your S-class PRSI contribution every year. You need an average of 48 payments (or credits if you were ill or unemployed) if you are to receive a full state pension. If you don't contribute your pension will be reduced.

Registration

Businesses have to have an assortment of relationships with agencies of the state: Companies Registration Office for either a business name or a company, The Revenue for taxes etc. There may be other relevant registrations you are required to have. You need to check the requirements in your industry and ensure you are compliant or you could get yourself into a heap of trouble.

Sales

This is a critical skill and there will be a section on the process but learn from other sources too.

Taxation

Already mentioned is registration for Income Tax and/or Corporation Tax. You may also have to register for VAT, Relevant Contracts Tax, or indeed as an employer (PAYE).

The semi-final stage in your self-education process is to create a set of **milestones** for the business. I think the most accessible way to do this is using these examples:

Start date minus 3 months

Milestone	Measured by
Research Phase	Information you have gathered
Start your own business course	Course Signed up for Probably a business plan started

Start date minus two months

Milestone	Measured by
Year 1 Business plan completed	Wallchart to Graph it in place
Website & Marketing materials ready	Domain name, Logo, business cards
Key Customers identified	List created, Contact method decided
Marketing plan initiated	First 10 preferred prospects contacted

Start date minus one month

Milestone	Measured by
Location identified	Lease in your possession ready to be signed
Business Registered	Docs submitted as required
Systems in place	First customers contacted Meetings, calls, Emails, orders

Start date minus three weeks

Milestone	Measured by
Mentor, Accountant and solicitor appointed	Named
Supports in place	Documented
Funding confirmed	Loan offers or money in bank

Start date minus two weeks

Milestone	Measured by
Bank account open	Card, chequebook in your possession, Online banking done
Insurance in place	Policy Document
Premises ready	Snag list complete
REALISTIC Sales and cash flow targets set for the next 6 months	Documented

Day one

Milestone	Measured by
First Sale made	Order in the bag (it is not day one till you make that sale)
Doors Open	Full schedule of work for the day

Start date Plus one month

Milestone	Measured by
Sales targets reached	Documented
First Cash flow Reviewed and amended	Reflecting what really happened as distinct from your projection
Books up to date	Documented
Pipeline established based on Marketing plan	Documented, (probably in your CRM software)
Regular Mentor Meetings	Minutes of meeting Outcomes measured
Problems being managed as they arise	Documented and solutions noted Learnings identified to avoid recurrence

Start date plus three months

Milestone	Measured by
Sales targets reached	Documented
Cash flow Reviewed and fewer amendments required than month 1	Reflecting what really happened as distinct from your projection
Books up to date	Documented
Marketing plan reviewed and updated in line with pipeline performance	Documented, (probably in your CRM software)
Regular Mentor Meetings	Minutes of meeting Outcomes measured
Problems being managed as they arise	Documented and solutions noted Learnings identified to avoid recurrence

These are clearly some generic milestones. You have to write them for your own business. Where I have suggested specific information for example cash flow, then numbers should be included in the milestone in order to make it more measureable.

You should write the table with an extra box to the right to compare what you thought would happen with the reality. It might lead to higher accuracy later. You should do the same with cash flow. What did it cost versus what you thought it would cost. Regrettably the real is very often higher than the expected.

Page 3:
The final part of the structured self-education is always blank at the start. It is for all the things you discover you don't know as you go along. However as the saying goes 'the more you know, the more you know you don't know'. So it grows over time and you need to make a plan for all the stuff you need to learn. It becomes in essence your Continuous Professional Development plan.

Every start-up business has issues. Because you have little experience you are likely to make a number of potentially very expensive mistakes. How do you prevent that? It's a normal part of your business education. Right? ***No not right.*** That's where having a mentor comes in. It doesn't matter if you pay them or they are just a more experienced business person that you talk to regularly. You need a mentor. A mentor holds up a mirror on your decisions with no agenda other than your success. A mentor should ask awkward questions to which you don't have the answers. A mentor should be the person you turn to when you are not sure who to call. Without your mentor what will you do to solve the problem you don't have the experience to deal with? You cannot do it alone.

There are mentor groups, like PLATO, where small business owners are supported by senior executives from multinationals. (*https://platodublin.ie*)

There are also business networking groups which, while focused on generating referrals, can often provide the right kind of connections to form a mentoring relationship. And, of course, there are professional mentors like me.

Even Enterprise Ireland and the LEO's provide a subsidised mentoring programme. This is about the ongoing learning every business owner needs to do. It is unstructured, demand driven CPD for business owners. Most important it provides an alternative voice and viewpoint and defeats some of the loneliness that is inherent in running your own business.

Once you choose a mentor, decide how often you need them and go from there.

Checklist of Educate Tasks

ACTION	☑
Sign up for a "Start Your Own Business" Course	☐
Audit of all that I Know	☐
Audit of All the things I need to learn	☐
Timeframe for the learning (Schedule the training over the first year of the business)	☐
Figure out who I will delegate to	☐
Sort out Milestones	☐
Get a mentor	☐

Chapter 3:
Arm Yourself

Find Support For Your Business
There are so many different strands of support available to a start-up that it would be madness to ignore them all. Why would you start a business and in essence ignore free investment?

Available funding and support boil down to these primary sources:

1. **Enterprise Ireland**
   if you fit the criteria – which most start-ups do not. The state recognised this and set up LEO's

2. **LEO** – your Local Enterprise Office

3. **DEASP** – Your local employment support

4. **Revenue (***https://revenue.ie***)**

5. **Other state supports**

As soon as a book is written it is out of date so check the referred websites to obtain the most up to date and accurate iteration of this information or go to:
https://supportingsmes.gov.ie/

1. Enterprise Ireland

Targets businesses with more than 10 employees or a turnover in excess of 1 million. They also have a focus on export (including internationally traded services) or manufacturing.

Because most start-ups don't meet the criteria there is instead the Local Enterprise Office (LEO). As this book is for start-ups I will just give the web link: *https://www.enterprise-ireland.com*

2. LEO *https://www.localenterprise.ie/*

Supports businesses with 1-10 employees, which is probably you. The enterprise must have potential for growth in domestic and/or export markets and also potential for new job creation.

Priority is given to exporters (including internationally traded services) or manufacturing. It is happy to support those people already trading. Applications for LEO support must be made prior to any expenditure being incurred.

Some of the more widely used LEO supports include:

Mentoring:
One-to-one meeting with experienced business mentors who will address issues with the business owner.

Trading Online Vouchers
Your LEO can contribute up to a maximum of €2,500 or 50% of the cost towards an e commerce enabled website and its marketing. (Must be 6 months trading and complete some training around this to qualify).

Feasibility Study/Innovation grant
You can get 50% of the costs of your market research, consultancy and your own labour among other things up to €15,000 ex VAT. Importantly, you don't have to pay back the money.

Priming Grant
Support of up to €15,000 (or 50% of salary) for each qualifying job you create, including your own job.

Business Expansion Grant
This is very targeted on manufacturing or internationally traded service business. They must employ one to ten people and the LEO has to believe that on growth, they will have the capacity to progress to the Enterprise Ireland portfolio. They offer €15,000 per job and a normal max of €80,000. Exceptional cases can be eligible for up to €150,000. All of these are subject to a maximum funding of 50%.

Innovation Vouchers
If your business is a limited company, you can apply for an innovation voucher worth up to €5,000. This is paid to a registered knowledge provider to do an agreed piece of work. For example, research or prototyping, or new product/process development, new business model development, innovation/technology audit.

Technical Assistance for Micro Exporter's Grant
This enables clients to explore and develop new market opportunities. It allows you to research export markets, e.g. exhibiting at Trade Fairs, preparing marketing material and developing websites specifically targeting overseas markets. Grant Covers 50% of eligible costs (net of vat) to a max of €2,500. This can be applied for once a year.

3. Department of Enterprise and Social Protection (DEASP) *http://www.welfare.ie*

Short Term Enterprise Allowance (STEA)

The Short-Term Enterprise Allowance (STEA) gives support to people who have lost their job and want to start their own business. It's paid instead of Jobseeker's Benefit for a maximum of nine months. It ends when the entitlement to Jobseeker's Benefit ends (that is at either nine or six months after you have received the first payment).

This payment is taxable

Back to Work Enterprise Allowance (BTWEA)

If you have been out of work and in receipt of social welfare for more than nine months, under the Back to Work Enterprise Allowance you can keep your social welfare payment for two years if you set up a business (year 1: 100% – year 2: 75%).

This payment is not taxable.

Enterprise Support Grant (ESG)

This is for participants on the above schemes has a maximum value of €2,500 (BTWEA) and €940 (STEA) towards specific expenses of the business. You cannot apply for this in relation to money already spent as the payment is made to the supplier by DEASP.

Jobs Plus

JobsPlus is an employer incentive that offers you financial support if you take on an unemployed person. JobsPlus offers up to €10,000. It is payable monthly. It is paid in relation to the employee rather than the job or role.

The Wage Subsidy Scheme
The Wage Subsidy Scheme provides financial incentives to employers to employ disabled people who work more than 20 hours per week.

4. Revenue *https://revenue.ie*
There are a number of incentives from revenue but they are always subject to change at budget time. They all have an expiry date which is sometimes extended. Check the web for the up to date position.

What is generally different about Revenue supports is that they reduce the amount of tax you pay. It can't go below zero so you might miss out.

Three-year Corporate Tax Exemption
Under this scheme, you can "technically" earn €120,000 in net profit without paying Corporation Tax in each of the first three years. The scheme gives relief from corporation tax on your trading income. There are some Terms and Conditions.

Start-up Refunds for Entrepreneurs (SURE)
This is for people who start a limited company and need cash to fund its growth. It allows you to claim back the income tax you paid on the money you are investing.

For example Last year I paid €1,600 in tax according to my P60. In the previous year I paid €4,500. All my tax was at 20%. If I am investing €10,000 in the business I can reclaim €2,000 under SURE (20% of the €10,000) from revenue. That's all of last year's tax and some of the previous year.

The Employment and Investment Incentive Scheme
This is identical to SURE but it is for people who might invest in your business from outside. You have to repay the investment after a period of at least four years. The investment must be in shares in the business.

R&D Tax Credit
This is to encourage investment by companies into research and development. The main challenge for SMEs is identifying what qualifies for this relief. You may need assistance with that. Ask your accountant or mentor.

Accelerated Capital Allowance
This is to encourage companies, paying corporation tax, to buy energy efficient equipment and machinery. You can write-off 100% of the purchase value of qualifying energy efficient equipment against your profit, in the year of purchase.

5. Other supports

Microfinance Ireland *https://microfinanceireland.ie/*
Microfinance acts as the bank of last resort. They offer loans at a reasonable cost to people who might not, for whatever reason get a loan from a bank. They offer different options from €2,000 to €25,000 usually repaid over 3 years.

Strategic Banking Corporation of Ireland *https://sbci.gov.ie*
Offers loans (€25,000 to €5 m) through the pillar banks and some finance houses for asset purchase at reduced rates of interest and over a longer term typically up to 10 years for larger loans

Credit Guarantee scheme
https://sbci.gov.ie/schemes/sme-credit-guarantee-scheme-cgs
Only available through Bank of Ireland and Ulster Bank. This is a guarantee to the bank for 80% of the outstanding balance of the loan should you default. It costs 2% extra and is to make lending lower risk for both sides.

Checklist of 'Arm Yourself' Tasks

ACTION	☑
Contact any of the relevant agencies	☐
See what hoops you need to jump through	☐
Find out the timeframe for accessing the funding or support	☐
Find a way to make that fit with your other timelines and action plans	☐
Amend and adjust things in line with the possibility of this funding.	☐

Chapter 4:
Driving The Business

The person who drives the business is you. The hat you wear while driving it depends very much on the type of person you are. Are you more the entrepreneur or more the manager? This was why I suggested earlier on that you take some of the personality tests, so that you could identify the potential for both success and for disaster that having you at the helm brings. Knowing that information may, or may not change the outcome.

I am not going to deal here with every nitty gritty bit of how you manage a business rather I hope to hit a few highlights.

Every person will do things in their own way. If you did the personal SWOT analysis I suggested in the action list on page 25 you are already aware of what problems you might face just based on the fact that it is you in control. In educating yourself you will mitigate that risk.

I suggest that at this stage, if you haven't done it already, you do a SWOT on the business and I want to introduce you to the concept of responding to SWOT in a practical way.

Lots of Entrepreneurs do SWOT but they really don't make any practical use of the information and that is a mistake. So here I want to present to you a simple practical use for the information you gain by doing a SWOT analysis.

As you look at the 2 matrices: something few people notice is that on the upper horizontal axis Strengths and Weaknesses are *internal*. This is something totally within your abiltity to control and change using the corresponding segment of the USED matrix.

On the lower horizontal axis, Opportunities and Threats are *outside* of ourselves and so harder to control.

If we look at the vertical axis we see that we have *positive* on the left and *negative* on the right. Which do you focus on? Which way did you view the illustration? Just be aware, there is no right or wrong answer to this.

SWOT, as you are already aware, is **Strengths, Weaknesses, Opportunities and Threats**. The Used Matrix is the direct action response to each of the pieces of information gathered and it requires specific action for each point. The Used Matrix is: **Utilise, Stop, Exploit and Defend.**

If you have a strength how do you propose to utilise that strength to best effect to grow the business? For every strength you have, there needs to be a corresponding way to use that strength otherwise what is the point identifying it in the first place.

With weaknesses it is the very same. For every weakness you need a strategy to prevent the potential damage that the weakness could cause to your fledgling business. The more established you are the less likely that the weaknesses impact you because you built a robust defence or better still eliminated them in the early stages of the process.

Opportunities are hard won and so it is very important to exploit every opportunity presented. Opportunity is not always something you have control of especially in terms of its timing. So you need to define a process that makes sure you do not unwittingly miss a golden opportunity. Once you put in place a process for capturing opportunities it becomes a habit. Need I say more?

 If you don't defend against the threats that present themselves then you are left vulnerable. Again here systematic defences are the way forward. Let's just look at how you might defend against a large competitor with a big budget available to ensure you don't damage his business. My opinion on this is to defuse the concept that you are a threat to them (even if they are a threat to you). Build a relationship. Play the role of the small fish that is willing to take the scraps from the big guys table. So you end up with work where you are endorsed by your largest competitor and they are introducing you to their customers. You are doing the work the competitor doesn't want to do and you, instead of competing with them, are dealing with their valued clients. Finding a win-win when you are threatened is a really good defence.

To drive the business you need a priority system. Which customer is the most important? What should be done first? What is the best use of my time right now? You need to manage your time in such a way that you are not just reacting to what happens but also you are getting some time that you can do planned actions. Time cannot be managed – it goes by irrespective. You *can* manage what you do while it flies by. What time of day are you most productive? Is there a time of day when you could choose not to be interrupted? Is there something in the business that it is just not possible to delegate, something ONLY YOU can do? These are the management decisions.

> **Nugget:**
> *What is the best use of*
> *my time – Right Now?*

In the same way you have to plan for replacing yourself when you don't have the time to do everything. You need to gradually list all the things you do; and in a perfect world, how you do it, so as to create job descriptions for the people who will replace you performing that task.

Automate anything you can, especially mundane stuff. There is a lot of innovative software out there to record client contact time and allow you to invoice it. Is there different way to do some of the basic tasks in your business? Do you have a new methodology for example, which might make you better? What would give you a unique edge over your competition? Don't do anything; in particular the mundane stuff, in the way it has always been done, unless it is the most efficient way you can do it. Look for ways to innovate, do things better, faster.

In *Driving the Business* too there are very specific relationships you might want to foster. Pick the three customers or potential customers that you want as your biggest accounts and work on the personal relationships. Build similar relationships with key suppliers, your bank manager and your advisor team (Mentor, Accountant and Solicitor). So that you can pick up the phone and they all take your call without question. For pointers on this I refer you to a book by a used car salesman. 'How to sell anything to anybody' by Joe Girard. A quote from Joe; '*Do first what's necessary, then what is desirable and suddenly you find you are doing what most people consider the impossible*'. It sums up driving the business for me. If at the end of each day you review what is necessary on the following day and make sure it will be done that will generate the space for the desired outcomes. It's often having the personal discipline to get it done that impresses the customer or influencer.

My last Driving point is that in driving the business you absolutely must have a clear vision on where the destination is. That's why you need a roadmap to plot the route from where you are now to where you want to be in one year, three years and five years. The really big corporations, like Toyota, have a 50 and 100 year strategy. Someone has to be the visionary, the leader if your business is to reach those milestones. This is why I repeat that you have to test and measure performance against a set of criteria. If you do not have something to aim at how will you hit it? You need, somewhere in the business plan, a Big Audacious Goal. Something you strive to achieve. It needs to be realistic and still be achievable, but at a stretch. The strategy that you then apply to achieving the goal should be measured regularly. It keeps your focus on the target, keeps your head in the game not just working in the business. We will discuss this at length in the next chapter.

Getting Paid

Business is about the money. So how will you ensure that your customer pays you? We kind of assume that if they buy they will pay. I am not a fan of assumptions. I would rather make sure. First you need a policy (a decision as to how will I do things) Will I offer credit? No would be my answer. You can't afford it. If you must do it you need proper terms which are agreed between the parties. A written agreement that is court enforceable. Oh yes; with credit the day will come that you find yourself in court because you were not paid. In your industry what is normal behaviour? Do you ask for a deposit like they do in the window or fitted kitchen business? If so how much? When do you expect to get paid? It is something you cannot leave to chance. The biggest reason people do not pay on time is because they don't get asked for the money on time. Indeed you could leave out the words *on time* here and you would probably see the reason people do not get paid.

Ask for the money.
You earned it.

One last thought on this: Cheques are almost gone, most payments are now either electronic or by card. So you need to explore the most financially beneficial way to be able to offer card payment. Is it Stripe?, Paypal? Could you use a machine from the bank? Would that be economic for you? There are so many options today where you don't even have to rent a machine. Look into all of this and make sure you can meet the customer expectations on how easy it should be to pay you.

Drive the Business, Checklist of actions

ACTION	☑
Do the relevant personality check	☐
Complete SWOT and USED on the business	☐
Look at all the roles in the business and develop job descriptions for when you can't do everything any more	☐
Build your priority system	☐
Build the priority Relationships	☐
Ensure that all compliance documentation is done and on time – systemise this	☐
Look for ways to systemise, automate mundane repeated tasks. Create a budget to do this	☐
Create your one, three and five year goals for the business and put them on the wall	☐
Sort out your Payment arrangements, terms of business	☐

Chapter 5:
Year 1 Business Plan

I can hear the resistance to the idea of writing a business plan as I write each sentence. **NOT writing a business plan would be a BIG mistake.** So here is the logic:

1. The Plan is the Roadmap I referred to in the last chapter
2. It is a living growing document that evolves as the business grows
3. It is informed by:
    a) what happens in the business and
    b) the management strategy used to achieve the aims and goals of the business
4. It is the means by which performance is measured
5. It is often the first iteration of website content

So let's deal with each of these points to generate a little enthusiasm.

1. The roadmap:
If you are talking to a financier or a bank they need to see that you know what you are at. They need to know that their investment is safe. So do you and your family.

You need to be confident that the risk you are taking in starting this enterprise is a well worked out, calculated risk.

You need to be able to see that you are not putting your future at risk and that, in fact, if you deliver on the promises in the plan, that you are likely to succeed or even exceed the financial milestones you set. You've laid out a deliverable action plan and there is no sense of *'it'll be grand'* as an attitude but rather that you are making sure that it happens pretty much according to plan. No surprises!

2. The evolving document.
After the first three months you know, based on the numbers alone, if you have enough customers buying enough from you to hit your projected marks. It doesn't actually matter whether you are up or down because you have learned what to do more of, or less of to put the plan on track. If it is exceeding expectations the only question is: what are we doing right? and how can we do more of the same? But tweak the document at least every quarter to add in or to take out whatever needs changing.

3. It responds to reality
Really, the evolution of the business forces you to re-think things or perhaps focuses you: in the areas you expected or perhaps in an area where you didn't expect to be focused. Recognise what has to change in response to the market and remember: 'It's bad luck to

> **Nugget**
> *Numbers never Lie. If it doesn't add up then either you must change it until it does add up or don't start the business.*

refuse profit'. My simple axiom is **Follow the money**. Put the effort into what is profitable and put aside the things that do not generate profits. Be absolutely ruthless. You cannot afford to do otherwise.

When you write stuff into a business plan you are saying: I intend to do that. You set up measurement points which are invariably numbers. Sales of *X*-thousand per month from *Y* number of customers. Or, *A* number of enquiries per week through the website with a conversion rate of *B* and an average value of *C* per sale. These are all measurable and if they are achieved the implication is that you planned very accurately or at least realistically. So comparing the reality with the plan can be either very satisfying or sobering and you will amend the numbers for the next period in response to what has happened.

It seems to me that we judge ourselves very harshly based on these numbers. It is a learning process. It might happen faster or slower than expected or the client you thought was over the line delays or some other thing messes up the plan. The only question is: What will I do about it? Nothing else is needed. Learn month by month and move forward.

4. The measurement tool

Yes, just basing measurement on the money is crude but any measurement is better than none. The simple question of how well did we think we would do versus what really happened helps you to learn. You are open to learning or you would not be reading this book. Now you are learning from your own mistakes or successes. The key question is WHY? Why did this event happen? Why did we gain or lose that customer? Why do we have more money in the bank than we expected? Or less? WHY? If you don't measure you don't compare. If you don't measure you just stagger from one problem to the next, never really in control.

5. The content for the web

Writing the persuasive text about the business is what your website is all about. You won't be able to just use the text from the business profile (from the business plan) because you need keywords and so on, but we will get to that later. The point is, you are making your real business virtual so that it becomes accessible online. What do you want people to say; to know; to think about your business? Get your message on song. Writing it down makes it real. So tell people – in the plan first, then a more detailed version for the web – what you want them to believe about your business. Then all you have to do is live up to the promises you make. Easy. Right?

Believing what you write about yourself and the business is your first step to success.

So let's look at the two versions of the plan. We will be really imaginative and call them Plan A and Plan B. You always need a plan B in case there is an issue with plan A.

So here is some typical content for a year-1 plan

Plan A (for others)		Plan B (for you)	
1	Executive Summary	1	Financials and graphs
2	Promoters Profile	2	Overall strategy
3	Business Profile & Structure	3	Market Analysis
4	Market Analysis	4	Marketing Plan
5	Marketing Plan	5	Business Profile & Structure
6	Overall strategy	6	Promoters Profile
7	Financials and graphs	7	Executive Summary

I will explain the differences further in.

Plan A

The plan should be no more than 10 pages and here is the key bit: The outsider will probably only read the executive summary and the numbers.

You however will have learned loads through the process of writing the document. You will notice the massive difference between the two versions of the plan! The key differences will be in what you decide to leave out in the version for outsiders.

1. The Executive Summary

This is positioned first and written last. It is stating in a single paragraph the content of each of the sections that follow it. It allows the reader to get the big picture in a one pager. That is why it is so important. You can't really write it until you have written the other pages so leave it till last.

2. Promoters Profile

The reader only knows what you write down so what do you need to tell them about you and what you bring to the party.

- What have you done in business in the past (either in a job or for yourself) Leave out nothing. You can edit later.
- Why did you pick this business to start with?
- Why is there such a good fit between you and this business?
- What is your expertise in this business?
- What contacts or possible customers do you bring?

- What roles will each person fulfil in the business? If it is just you what parts of the business will it be smart for you to subcontract out?

Answer the following two questions for each person who is an owner in the business:

- What is the most impressive thing about you?
- Why are you the perfect person to lead this enterprise?

As you write this you will find that you have additional detail and content to add to the personal SWOT and USED analyses.

This content should also inform a lot of changes (or alignment) in the profiles you have created on any social media platforms you operate. (Twitter, LinkedIn, Instagram, Facebook) These profiles need to offer a consistent message. If you appear a serious business person on one platform and a party animal on another how will you be perceived by potential customers, suppliers, influencers around the business? This applies equally to the personal and to the business profile: What you put up is the public face of the business. That is the basis people use to form their opinion of you and your business. If you choose to put nothing up, people will form opinions anyway and you will not have had the opportunity to influence that opinion.

3. Business Profile & Structure

This section will seriously help you to define your message to the customer. It needs to include the relevant information that would cause a possible client to want to know more about the business. I will say a lot more about this in the marketing section. In the meantime here are some questions this segment should answer:

- What do you do? First a list then in Fair Detail
- How do you do it?
- Where do you currently do it?
- How much do you charge?
- How is the business to be structured?
- Who does what in the business?
  - Management
  - Sales
  - Marketing
  - Planning
  - Finances

Create an organisational chart if it simplifies things

4. Market Analysis

If you did the research work from chapter one you already have most of the work done for your market analysis. The aim of your market analysis is to get proof that there is customer demand. When you have competitor research it allows you to strategically position your business in the overall marketplace. This research means that you understand, in detail, what is going on.

This segment of the business plan also shows *you* how much you have learned.

5. Marketing Plan

I was taught very young that all the knowledge – or indeed all the talent – in the world is useless if you don't do something with it. You have gathered all the information; you understand what is happening, how the customer is behaving. Now you can write a simple list of measureable actions to communicate your specific message to each of your target customer types. Once you have tested and measured the impact of that communication and followed up with let's say the first ten targets you know how to tweak the actions to improve results. This is your marketing plan in its simplest form. I know who I want. What am I doing to achieve the result? Is it working?

6. Overall strategy
This is your big picture thinking. Where do you vision the business in 3 years' time? And how do you propose to measure that achievement?

I always say that numbers never lie so it should probably be in net profit retained in the business, (sustainable net profit multiplied by 7 is the easiest way to value a business for sale). You could equally measure it in your salary or lifestyle improvement over where you are now. You could even notice the number of people employed, the earnings per staff member, the number of customers, average value per transaction or simply the sales graph per month.

You have to have the information gathered in the first place, otherwise you have nothing on which to measure business performance.

Now you know the direction, you need to decide on the strategic actions to take in order to make that happen? How many people will it take? What structures do you need in place? A simple action plan with timelines and targets is enough as long as you can measure.

7. Financials and Graphs

All of this information we have been trying to capture and communicate needs to be reflected in easy-to-interpret pictures. All the background figures should be there: Cashflow Projection, Profit and Loss, Balance Sheet.

I suggest a graph of the numbers. Here is an example of a profit graph. It is measured quarterly over a period of years and allows you to capture the information at a glance.

You can see big peaks and troughs settling down to a much less extreme pattern. You take that in in seconds rather than ploughing through figures.

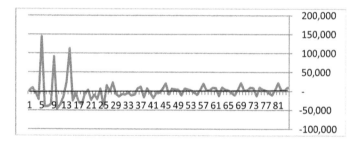

I hope you already see how helpful a graph can be to you the owner as you try to understand the numbers.

Look next at the income line (next graph). In the early months the expenses are greater than the sales but as the year goes on things improve. It is clear there is a seasonal dip and then a ramp to the most profitable part of the year. While the business needs cash flow support up as far as month eight, it can support itself on its own after that. That is how easy the graph makes the numbers.

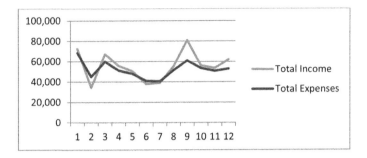

This business owner, yes it is real, needs to demonstrate how and why she will achieve the indicated turnaround if the bank is to support her. The text in the executive summary is what does that.

Most banks read the Executive Summary and the figures and if these two stand up then they read the rest. If not then the likely answer is No.

If you write the plan based on the methods used here then you have to believe what you write. That means simply that if it doesn't add up then either you must change it until it does add up or don't start the business.

Plan B
The difference between plan A and Plan B is the start point. I've described plan A so far but I gave you a big hint in chapter one as to the fundamental difference in my approach. You can't write Plan B without the research. Plan B doesn't start with the business. It starts with *you*. The purpose of the business is to provide for *you* all your material needs.

Step 1 is to figure out how much it costs you to live for a year. You do that by first completing the MABS budget sheet *(page 25)*. From here on in the construction of the business plan almost completes itself.

You now have very clear targets. Instead of trying to estimate how much the business can make in profit you now have a number which it ABSOLUTELY MUST make in profit. That number is the one generated by the budget. The business must first and foremost, support you. Otherwise it is a hobby not a business.

The impact of this is to totally invert the business planning process and it allows us to be driven by the numbers and it bears repeating: Numbers never Lie.

Let's do an example to illustrate: I am assuming it is a service business and that the numbers are all excluding VAT which I will address in the tax section.

Assume this: your number from the budget comes out at €36,000 a year (the average industrial wage). You have estimated that the business overheads are €9,000. So total sales required for the year are €45,000. I will digress slightly here and say that we need to stress test the business as part of this process so I am basing your earning capacity on the number of days per year you can earn multiplied by the minimum daily earnings required.

The formula is **WW x ED x RD = V**
Working weeks x Earning Days x Rate per Day = Viability.

In Ireland, for most businesses, you can expect to earn 45 weeks a year. I calculate this based on the following assumptions:

- There are 9 bank holidays a year. That's 2 weeks
- Between Dec 17 and Jan 10 you cannot expect

to earn. (if you do, it is a bonus and you should charge a premium rate for it) 3 weeks
- Allow one week for a break or holiday
- Allow one week for all the unforeseen things that happen in life in a year: weddings, funerals, doctors / vet appointment, school play, man flu, waiting for the plumber to fix a leak

In total that is 7 weeks lost. So in our example the €45,000 has to be earned in 45 weeks. In your head you are thinking yeah but… What if you budget on 48 weeks and you only earn 45 weeks? Nightmare. If you budget 45 and you are right and you earn 48 then I'm wrong but you are happy with an extra €3,000 in profit.

Now to the days per week: I have no doubt that you will work on at least 6 days a week to start but I contend that you won't get paid for all of them. In fact as the business grows I have found that most business owners end up spending less and less of their time working IN the business and more and more working ON the business doing things for which we don't get paid. For example you will use time on marketing, quotations, website stuff, social media, VAT returns, after sales service, meetings, travelling and so on. So in our formula I suggest budgeting based on FOUR earning days per week. If you earn for 5 that is great, but budget for 4.

So our Formula now reads:
45 weeks x 4 days = 180 earning days per year. €45,000 divided by 180 means your average earnings per day have to be €250. If you can achieve that then you have Viability. Most people have to figure that HOW out.

We will explore this in way more detail in the marketing section but here is the taster so that you can see how differently the business plan shapes up.

If I need €250 a day and my average sale is €50 then I need to sell to 5 people every day. If I am to do that my marketing probably has to bring me in front of 15 people a day. I need to create a series of measurable actions to ensure that I get to see those 15 people. To use the jargon that is 15 qualified leads per day. So I create the marketing plan to do that. Now I have to convert 15 conversations into 5 sales. I need a sales strategy to deliver my 5 sales a day. So my initial research tells me who and where the clients are and my marketing generates the leads to hit the sales target to deliver the numbers we have to earn. We have solid measurable targets rather than a best guess number. That is why we turn the business plan upside down. It is based on what I MUST do rather than what I Might do. That is why Plan B should really be Plan A.

> **Nugget**
>
> *Sustainable net profit multiplied by 7 is the easiest way to value a business for sale.*

Business Plan checklist

ACTION	☑
Assess how much I need to earn for a year	☐
Break that down across the formula to a number of sales per day	☐
Write up the marketing plan and sales strategy	☐
Build the rest of the business plan around that formula to create an absolute number	☐
Write the plan based on this rather than imagination	☐
Assess the viability of the business and modify the plan till it works - or accept the fact that it doesn't and abandon the project seeking something that won't break your heart instead.	☐

Part Two

Aim

> **Nugget:**
> *The purpose of a business is to provide for you, all your material needs.*

Aim

This section is very much the nitty gritty stuff of running a business and I hope you will be able to come back to this section again and again for a refresh on ideas or to clarify things. It is the reference section of the book because the three sections are all things you will use every single day. It is not exhaustive on any of the sections. Each could be and probably is a book in its own right. So consider this my edited highlights, the stuff I think you have to know.

Accounts

These are the weapon of choice for measuring performance. This is the ultimate crash course. I believe that if you know the numbers, from entering them up on a system every week you have your hand on the heartbeat of your business. That is why I strongly encourage you to keep your own accounts, at least in the early stages. By doing so you will learn to understand what is going on in the business below the surface.

Internet

This is now one of the main routes to market for most small businesses because that is where most people look for a service provider. For that reason alone you have to have an internet presence. We will look at just some of the ways you can use the internet to create awareness, market, sell, gather information and measure the performance of what you do online.

Marketing

You can do a degree in marketing. I don't have one so there are much more expert people than me on the topic but you need the basics and I am including a few of my quirkier ideas for reaching your customer here. Without marketing you do not have customers and without customers you do not have a business. That's why the marketing chapter is the longest one in the book.

Chapter 6:
Accounts

I suspect that in spite of its importance to the business this will be the least read chapter in the book. Lots of people miss a trick here and slow the growth of their business dramatically for lack of key information. I said it in regard to research: Information is power. In regard to accounts that goes double.

Maria von Trapp (Julie Andrews in The Sound of Music) says that the beginning is a very good place to start so let's go there. When I teach this to a group I always promise we can do the whole thing in one minute. I hope you read quickly.

The first account we need to mention is the business bank account. There is no escaping it. You need a separate bank account for the business. It means your money and the business's money are different. When you transfer money from the business to your personal account then you can spend it on whatever you want. But the business bank account is just for the money you spend on behalf of the business. This arrangement keeps everything really clean in the event that revenue ever decides to audit you.

To set up your records the first thing you need is a big Nail. Once you have driven that nail through a board or something similar you are ready. Every time you buy something for the business get a receipt and put it face down (so that the sunlight doesn't fade it) on the nail, something like the photo below. If you don't do that an accountant will charge you around €40 an hour to sort the mess of receipts and enter the information. At the end of every month, while you still remember what each expense is for, take them off the spike and file them. Then you need to enter them in a book or a spreadsheet. When you total up the spreadsheet, adding in any direct debits, (for things like phones, insurance and utility bills), loan repayments and so on from the bank statement, you now have a monthly money out total.

You have been doing invoices for your customers all month so you know who paid and who still owes you. That's the money in total.

Date	No	Payee	Details	INCOME		EXPENSES							
				Bank	Total	Pur-chases	Esb-Gas	Draw-Ings	Pho-Ne	Motor	Admin	Ads-Mkt	Loan
Jan													
6	1	ESB	Bill				200						
11	2	Supplier 1	Materials Customer 1			350							
14	Inv 21	Customer 1		750									
15	POS	Motor Tax								160			
18	POS	Garage	Diesel							50			
24	DD	Google ads										100	
28	Inv 22	Customer 2		1,800									
30	Inv 23	Customer 3		1,500									
31	DD	Loan											450
31	EFT	personal a/c	My Drawings					1,761					
31	DD		Mobile bill						70				
				4,050		350	200	1,761	70	210	0	100	450

Money IN less money OUT tells me how much is left – Profit. And there is the first stage of accounts done in 150 words. It really is not rocket science. If you can do that you are well on the way. You know the numbers.

If you are not keen to do it yourself, is there a family member with a bit of cop-on? I had a 9-year-old back in the day who could do it easily for a small fee, of course. You might have someone similar. Truthfully if an intelligent 9-year-old can do it so can you. It will give you a sense of control of the business and in my experience a sense of satisfaction. It also means that when tax return time comes around and all of your peers are panicking you are stress free because it is done.

In an ideal world you pay as you go for everything. So no one owes you anything and you owe nothing. Life is not always like that so you need to keep a tight track on that. That is called credit control. Personally I don't think that most start-ups can afford to offer credit so it is a topic you should openly discuss with your customers.

This is the first complication: If you are giving or receiving credit you have to include that in your money in money out total. So it is cash in plus money owed to me less cash out and money I owe. That is the truthful figure.

The next wrinkle is VAT. If your total sales for the calendar year are less than €37,500 then you do not have to register for VAT and this section will not apply to you. If you have to register then you have to record VAT separately. You will need 3 columns on the spreadsheet Total, Value (excluding VAT) and VAT. You need that on both the money in and money out sides. Now you also have a record of how much

VAT you paid, from the invoices you received. How much VAT you charged, from the invoices you sent. The difference must be paid to Revenue every two months. Doing the paperwork is still just a case of getting used to doing it every month.

If you look at the sample spreadsheet *(page 75)* you will see how easy this is. You can extract everything you need from this simple sheet. It doesn't need to be any more complicated than that. If you use an excel sheet then you can get it to do all the calculations for you and that is very convenient.

Most important of all is the understanding of what the accounts tell us about the health or not of the business. It will show you very quickly what you are spending, what you spend it on. Are you spending more this month than last? You will see trends up or down. You may spot opportunities to reduce costs which is another way to improve profitability.

Many people see accounting as some kind of black art. It isn't. It is just that it is outside most people's experience. The sample basic spreadsheet (on page 75) has typical entries.

You can change the headings to suit your business. You could add a column on each side for VAT if that were applicable to your business.

Just doing this every month, or every week if that fits better for you, keeps you in full control of what is happening in your business. That helps to keep the stress of managing the business to a minimum leaving you focused on where the business is going rather than worried and out of control.

In a similar way it will show you who your good customers are. Most businesses get 80% of their revenue from 20% of the customers. Looking at the accounts you will see who the 20% are. Indeed you will probably also identify who you don't want as your customer because while you are busy with them you are making little or no profit.

You will also see trends month to month in terms of products or services selling well – or not and this should allow you to plan marketing to fill the holes that low sales might cause.

In regard to accounts the question I get asked most is what you should pay through the business? Some of the things you currently pay become business expenses once you start the business.

In addition to the obvious business expenses you can pay the following too from your business bank account:

- One third of Electricity and heat at home, assuming your home is your base, mailing address, or office. Do this by paying two of the six bills per year.

> **Nugget:**
> *To decide if a business expense is tax allowable; ask yourself: Was it for the benefit of the business?*

- Your broadband – which is essential for the business – in full because that is what it costs and it's not like electricity, you are not charged in terms of usage.
- Your mobile phone. Get on a fixed, all-inclusive tariff that is not usage based. It will be cheaper and your personal use is covered by the business.
- One waste bill per year.

How you treat motor expenses depends on a few details.

- If you have a commercial vehicle used for the business then generally everything you spend is paid through the business. If you use it sometimes for personal stuff then you need to keep track of how much of the use is for personal miles. A rough percentage is enough.
Say it is 10% of €1,000 annual motor expenses (€100) you must add that €100 to your profit at the end of the year for the purpose of calculating tax.
- If you use your own car then you can use the same system as for the commercial vehicle OR
- You could bill the business the civil service rate for business kilometres (between 21c and 83c per km depending on size of vehicle and how much travel you do in a year). Look here: *https://revenue.ie/ en/employing-people/employee-expenses/travel-and- subsistence/civil-service-rates.aspx*
- If you use your own car and you don't claim depreciation or capital allowances on the vehicle, you are making it available to the business for free. That saves the business the cost of buying a car and allows you to pay all the running costs through the business.

One of the questions I get asked regularly is what about depre- ciation. What is depreciation? It is the inevitable reduction in value as an asset gets older. You pay €25,000 for a new car. A year later it is worth €18,000. The year

Nugget:

Money is the oil that lubricates the engine of business. Let it run low and see what happens

after that €14,000 and so on over the years. Depreciation is dealt with by revenue as capital allowances and I will deal with that later. You only depreciate things that cost over €400. The rest you treat as disposable items and put them in as expenses in the current year.

There are two things to understand here. First is that the car loses 25% of its value in the first year (although Revenue only allow you to reduce its value by 12.5% for tax purposes). Second: wouldn't it be smarter to buy (or lease) a one year old car for €18,000.

I want to do an accounts comparison to demonstrate why, if you need to buy big ticket items, it makes more sense to lease them than to get a loan and buy them.

Let's suggest you need a printer, photocopier scanner that does 20 pages a minute and that machine costs €9,000.

The Loan option:
You borrow €9,000 over 3 years at 6.8% interest.

36 payments	€277 per month	€3,324 per year
Interest	€975 over 3 years	€325 per year

The amount Revenue allows you to write off against tax liability each year is:

Revenue allows 12.5% of the €9,000.	Interest Paid	Total allowed
€1,125	€325	€1,450

But you paid €3,324 over the year for the machine that means you have to pay income tax, PRSI and USC on the difference between what you paid and what is allowed. It totals €1,874. When I work it out, assuming you pay tax at 20% and PRSI and USC, It makes an extra tax cost of €534 per year or two extra payments.

If you lease the item and pay €32 per thousand per month:

36 payments	€288 per month	€3,456

It appears at first glance to be €146 more per year. However, when you take the tax of €534 into account you are up €388 because the entire €288 per month is tax allowable. In addition, if you are registered for VAT there is an further reclaim of nearly €54 per month, €648 a year. Even if you are not VAT registered at the start, you can claim this €54 from the first month you do register.

So while the gross payment looks marginally more you can see that in the end it costs between €300 and €1,000 less annually. Even if the 'why' of this doesn't make sense to you, believe me when I tell you; Leasing costs less than Hire Purchase or a loan because it is more tax efficient. It is also way more tax efficient than using your cash to just buy the asset. So it cost €9,000 but you have to add the tax etc. that you paid on that €9,000. You had to earn €12,500 before tax, PRSI and USC to have that €9,000. In addition you would use up cash that could be important for some other need or project later. The bigger the price the bigger the saving.

> **Nugget:**
> *Mistake...*
> *To get a loan for a big-ticket purchase when leasing is much more tax effective*

Accounts Checklist

ACTION	☑
Get a Nail	☐
Get some Files or envelopes to store what comes off the nail each month	☐
Set aside an hour a month when you can enter the information	☐
Set up a book or a spreadsheet similar to the one above	☐
Just Do It	☐

Chapter 7:
Internet

The internet is a vast topic. Hundreds of books, courses, videos, tutorials and webinars are written every year. It is now the biggest service industry in the world, turning over billions every month. I cannot hope to cover such a huge array of information in one chapter so I will instead try to hit some highlights to get you started.

Marketing is such a minefield. Online marketing has a huge array of options. I am going to address just three areas:

1. Basic web presence
2. Online advertising
3. Social Media

As I am not an expert in any of this you have to take it for what it is worth.

1. Getting Online

There is no question of being in business without a web presence. Even the most basic business needs to be online today simply because that is where customers look for suppliers.

If you want to be in the marketplace most of it is online today so what can you do? First the choice of a domain name – *www.something.ie* – to identify you as Irish. Ideally it should be something that describes what you do in the shortest easiest words you can think of. I like things like *painters.ie* or *micksgarage.ie*. Next go and get a website built. There are hundreds of providers in the business and obviously look them up online but don't just take them at their word. Go and talk to people who used them What were the pitfalls and issues? Select the person you trust.

You have to decide about the visual imagery and the text you are putting up. Here is the research I suggest you do: (Sorry for repeating this but think it has a different use here) Ask any 20 people what they would put into a search engine (Google, Bing, Wiki and so on) in order to find a business like yours. Once you find out what they would put into a search engine do it and see who comes up. Now you know who is getting the leads you want. Your site will consist of several pages. The landing page is the page usually referred to as 'Home'. On that page you want images and text that holds the person before they bounce to some other site. This is the toughest part of building a website, putting in content that holds the person's attention. Images, colours and text are all important. Revert to your business plan and start with the content of the business description there.

In order for people to find you there are things you have to do. Tweak your home page text so that the words the person used to find you (the search word or keyword) appear five or six times in the text. You will need all the images to have text tags because search engines do not find pictures they only find text. This is the very basic part of what is called Search Engine Optimisation or SEO. There is much more to it than this and as a result you will need help from another book or from a person more expert than I am. One thing that helps you get on page one; and let's face it very few people go beyond the first page in any search, is links with more established websites. These sites have been around for longer and are therefore more credible it seems. You need as many of these backlinks as possible to help your credibility with the search engines. An easy way to get some is to submit your information to free directory sites. There is a list of some of these among the appendices at the back of this book.

People do business with other people not with firms. The face behind the business is very important so in your 'About Us' page you need a short profile of the people behind the business. A photo or two helps a lot.

You will need to continuously update content or the site goes stale in the eyes of the search engine and you drop down the rankings.

Create a nice 'Contact us' page with all the contact details possible on it. Put in a web link so that people can send a message. Insert a captcha on this to defend against automated spam.

The most important thing on the website is to decide what you want people to do once they have visited. Will they buy from your online shop? Do you want them to call you? What will you do to encourage them to sign up for e mail newsletters / marketing? Why should they give you their e mail address? These are all the tools you could use to generate sales leads but they only work if you plan them into the website at day one. To do that you have to ask yourself, in advance, what do I want my website to do? Is it supposed to generate business? I think it should. So you need some kind of call to action on each page, whatever action you want the person to take.

As long as your site has the capacity for e commerce you may be eligible for significant financial support from your LEO to help with the cost of the site, and its SEO and advertising *(page 40)*.

2. Online advertising

If your website is not "organically" on the first page of the search engine you can pay to get it there. At its simplest you pay a fee for the key word. So for example If you sold first communion clothes you might pay anything from 10c to €5 for someone to click on your ad which takes them into your website. When I checked communion clothes there were no ads but on communion dresses there were four. This process is called pay per click (PPC). You set the cost of a click and the maximum value per day in total that you will spend. If you bid 80c per click and I bid €1 my ad will appear before yours. After your daily budget is exhausted your ad will no longer appear. You can control the geography where your ad is seen right down to a radius of your premises. You can even pick the time of day at which your ad can appear. You can run several different ads at the same time and see which one is working. They will give you dashboards and reports to show what is happening with the ad(s). Then you can fine-tune the target or content of the ad in order to get the potential client to do what you want them to do. It takes some practice to get this right so you should either limit your spend in the beginning or get help. The search engines will offer you on line help and will even talk to you to help you to make your campaign more effective.

There are whole businesses out there who are expert in the business of online ads, creating content, images and managing your entire campaign. They are in business and good luck to them. I believe you have to learn this stuff kinaesthetically. You have to do it yourself. Make the phone calls, create the content, choose the boundaries and budgets, get the advice and either follow it or not. This experience can only be measured on a Yes or No scale. It either works or it fails to work. No middle ground. If it is not working stop doing it. I know that sounds obvious but I've seen lots of people keep hoping it will work and keep on throwing good money after bad. '*I'll just give it one more week!*' So I am saying it – "Test and measure and only do the things that work."

As I was researching this segment of the book every website I visited had cookies to track me and send me specific customised ads. I'll be honest as a consumer, I'm not a fan. I find it too invasive, too pushy and I tend to say no to everything. Most people do not realise that every keystroke you type while logged into your google account is tracked to better understand your buying habits and send you more ads. You could do this and be one of those extremely accurately targeting advertisers. With the help of people like google; perhaps.

3. Social Media
Start by deciding what social media platform is right for you. Just because you have a personal Facebook page doesn't mean that it's the right platform for your business.

Here are a few questions to help you to decide which platforms suit your business.

- Which platform does your target customer use? You can find most of this information on line.
- You need to look at whether you are B2B or B2C. B2B probably means LinkedIn is your number one and Twitter number two
- B2C is more likely to be Facebook and then Instagram but do your own researches before you sign up
- Only sign up for the ones you can give the time to. How much time can you afford to spend in the medium term to foster critical online relationships?
- Create a time budget and consider automating some of the pieces but NEVER automate responses or follow-backs. Personalise these
- Be careful whose content you re-post or like. You will be associated with those people by your action
- How much content can you reasonably expect to put up each day, week, month?

> **Nugget:**
> *Online: New content is GOLD.*

Again all of this is time. It comes under the marketing heading. How many followers/likes do you need to have to create sufficient critical mass to generate real business? What will you need to do to get that number of followers?

- When putting up a post you need to decide what day of the week and what time of day will have the best impact for your business?

This is about when your customers go online most regularly. (*e.g. Case study 1 on page 15*)

There is a whole new race of people in the world now called social media influencers. The majority seem to be aiming themselves at the young (under 30) market. This is a totally new aspect of the online marketplace and if you think it might work for you; then you need a plan to become connected to and supported by these influencers. Find out what the cost of endorsement by these people will be. You need to put this in the marketing budget.

Many of the social media sites: Facebook, Twitter, Instagram will allow you to tune your ads to age, demographic, location, gender and so on in order to help you to reach the audience that you are targeting. Use it. It works. Again, there are hundreds of experts in the field of Social Media and I have barely scratched the surface here. You will have to read more or watch infomercials the same as I do. This entire internet topic is growing every day.

There are start-ups out there who don't have the budget to do most of what I suggest in this chapter but you can start with a micro site, available via some of the directory sites – e.g. *www.whatswhat.ie*, for as little as €50 a year. Don't avoid it because it is outside your comfort zone. That avoidance would be the biggest deepest hole you could step in in the era of on line selling.

I found one link that I feel is worth checking out in terms of social media information. I hope it is still there when you look:

https://khoros.com/resources/social-media-demographics-guide

I'm going to save the whole area of e mail marketing and content marketing for the next chapter. It is after all part of both chapters.

Internet Checklist

ACTION	☑
Get your focus group together and ask them: what they want to see on your webpage What they would google if searching for you What they would buy, or not buy from what you currently offer Why they would or would not buy	☐
Write your web text in line with what you learned AND from the readers viewpoint	☐
Write the business profile for the business plan if it is not already done and compare with the web text	☐
Create your professional social media profiles, making sure they all correspond on message with the website	☐
Decide carefully who to follow and who to like / repost	☐
Fit it into whatever number of time slots you need to make it pay	☐
Plan your advertising campaign – use it on a test and measure basis to ensure it returns sales	☐
Update web content regularly	☐
Create a Time Budget to do all of this	☐

Chapter 8:
Marketing

Again, there are books, and good ones, by the dozen on *mainstream* marketing theory and practice so I will try to be as disruptive as possible in what I present here. These are all things I believe, and have tried and tested over years. So this chapter is about ideas that I found that worked.

Marketing is not the same as sales. Here is the core difference: marketing creates the desire. Sales make it a reality.

Marketing, for me, resembles a market gardener with six big glasshouses. On the first day he goes out and clears a section of the first glasshouse, brings it to market, sells it and the returns to his glasshouse, fertilises the ground and re-plants it. Second day he moves on and repeats exactly

the same process. He repeats the process each day, moving from one glasshouse to the next. When he reaches the end of the sixth glasshouse what he knows is that enough time has passed and the first glasshouse is ready again.

Simply put; in his business and in yours; you have to plant something every day if you are going to harvest something every day. Once you accept that; it is only a case of what you plant and where you plant it. Not everything will grow to the same standard but if you plant enough there will be enough business there.

Marketing costs money! You need a budget to create awareness and get the customer in the first place. You also need a budget to retain customers. The budget should be about 5% of the sales you want to make. Sales of €45,000 require a budget of €2,000 to €2,500.

So let's start with the fundamentals: The experts say that there are four, six or seven P's (depending on the expert) that influence the buying decision. So here are *all eight* suggested with my particular twist. Really all this is about is dealing with the things that might stop them from making the buying decision.

> **Nugget:**
>
> *The reason most small businesses fail is lack of sales.*
>
> *The reason for the lack of sales is that nobody knows about the business.*

1. *Product* – and their desire for it.
   Why would a target client want to buy what you want to sell? If you have to educate your customer in terms of why they should buy, it makes your marketing process different,

compared to marketing something that they already want.

2. *Place* – Is it easy to buy? Is it accessible? Can they buy it on line?

3. *Price* – Where is your product on the Price -vs- Value continuum? Are you "cheap and cheerful" or are you the "exclusive", very expensive option?

4. *Positioning* – How do they perceive your product in terms of desirability? Are you as attractive to them as they are to you? Are you economy, budget or exclusive in terms of customer perception?

5. *Promotion* – Where do they hear about you? Through what channels? How often? What do they perceive their relationship with your business to be? "Word of mouth" is *not* promotion. *You* don't do it, you can't depend on it, you have no control over it (good or bad) so it can't be part of your marketing strategy.

6. *Packaging* – This isn't just the wrapper on a product. It is that, of course, but it is also about how the customer experiences interaction with your business. What is the customer experience like? Would it cause them to want to return and become raving fans?

7. *People* – This is the real core of good marketing for any product or service. People buy from people. Having the right staff meeting the client makes a huge difference to the likelihood of repeat or referred business.

8. *Performance* – How did the business perform? Was the product or service delivered as promised? Early? Late? Did service exceed

expectations or was it below par? How do you measure that performance?

Some combination of some or all of these factors influences the client to buy or not buy. Because you have thought about it you will unconsciously have developed a strategy to manage all of these factors in advance of starting the business. Write that strategy down and pop it into the business plan and there it is: your overall market strategy. It is the picture you choose to paint. It is how you choose to be perceived by your desired clients. An image of your business will emerge whether or not you do this. If you do it this way you control that image. People see what you want them to see – your business in its best light.

This feeds your marketing plan. This plan can be a combination of many different methods. Your choice of methods should be the things that you have tested and found to work effectively.

When I work with a business the strategy I fear most is a classic mistake represented by the two pictures below:

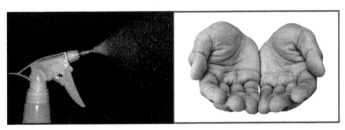

It is very common where people haven't thought it through. They just put out a website and some publicity and promotion material and hope the phone will ring. It is commonly called '*Spray and Pray*'. It is not a marketing strategy it is a *promotional* strategy. I will go as far as to say: ***It is only really marketing when there is a clear, measureable, prolonged result required from the activity.*** So first identify the outcome (syrategy) and then decide what to do in order to achieve it (tactics).

Nugget

Marketing is the communication of a specific message to targeted businesses or individuals with the express intention of encouraging them to buy.

Some of the marketing methods I've found that work better than *Spray and Pray* are rather more tactical. Here are a few of my favourite Guerrilla Marketing ideas with a comment on each one.

- **Marketing calendar.** This puts your name in front of your client every day for a year. It is an effective way to remind them you are there but it needs to be supported with more than that
- **Business card.** This should be used like confetti. Give everyone two cards. Tell them it is one to keep and one to give away
- **Signs** inside/outside/ on a vehicle. With your corporate brand or logo these just create awareness of you. There are many types of signs. You have to pick and of course test it and measure the effectiveness
- **Community involvement** is often ideal. Sponsoring a local team's jerseys or signage by the pitch can all have big impact on those involved in the club and their wider circle

- **The freebie**. What could you give away at little or no cash cost to you that would be a reminder to your potential customer?
- **Direct mail** letters. Nobody writes letters any more so this is a novel idea. I have done this many times and I always include something as an attention grabber which is referred to in the letter. Things I have included: An eraser, a band aid, a tea bag, a sachet of coffee even a photocopy of a €50 note. All worked in different ways with different results. What could you put in?
- **E-mail**: is effective if the content is good. Creating good content with an effective message is something you learn by doing. It is test and measure again. Never send out more than 10 of anything until you have tested it for response. That way you don't burn the whole list in one go. This applies to letters and e mail
- **A uniform** or branded workwear is both tax efficient and a useful awareness raiser
- **Contact time** with customer. There is no substitute for fostering a personal connection with the client. They are sure to buy from you if they consider you a friend. It changes them from a "Transactional Customer" to a "Relational Client"
- **Article in a publication**. This establishes you as a subject matter expert. So you are the authority.
- **Gift certificates** are great. Offer them. Especially since half of them are never redeemed. It is good marketing and free money
- **Networking**. Imagine that in your phone or on your Facebook page you have three hundred

people. Most people know at least 300 people. How many would be on a wedding invite list for example? So if you have 300 and they all know 300 each that's a potential customer base of 90,000. If you attract even half of one per cent of those it is 450 people. If they all spent €100 a year with you that is the €45,000 we discussed a few chapters ago

- **Opportunities to upgrade.** This is the deluxe option we discussed earlier
- **Testimonials** either written, or even better video on your website, are a real point of persuasion for potential clients. If an existing customer says it then it carries much more weight than if *you* say it
- **Reputation** springs from those testimonials. A reputation for under-promising and over-delivering is powerful and takes time to build. A reputation for honesty is very important. What reputation will you build?
- **Enthusiasm & Passion** is infectious. It will deliver customer satisfaction
- **Being easy to do business with** is the most powerful marketing you could do
- **Service** is back to the under promise idea. One of my past clients calls to customers 6 months after a job is complete just in case. It is a powerful marketing idea
- **Follow-up** with potential clients as many times as you need to. If you are submitting a price; be the last person to do so. It gives you a real (if slightly unfair) advantage when discussing your price with the client

I promised to deal with the area of **e-mail marketing** and there is just one thing you **MUST** do whatever you are writing. (I hope I've done it in this book).

> **Nugget:**
> *The best businesses don't try to create a demand. They see a demand, or need, and provide what the customer wants*

You need to use AIDA
AIDA is of course an acronym.
Attention You need some kind of headline, attention grabber, like the object in the envelope that causes the reader to become curious. Each line should make the reader want to read the next line (how am I doing?).

Interest Now that you have the reader's attention you have to hold it long enough to bring their attention to the actual content, sufficient to make them want something from the interaction. You want them to keep reading. In a flyer, for example, it might be an offer; in an e mail or a web page, something to get them to scroll down.

Desire happens once you have peaked the interest. It might just be a desire to know more so often the writer leaves something important out. This forces the reader to the last stage.

Action is what you actually want them to do. Go to the website, where the text is also written with AIDA in mind so it is leading them to a buy decision or a call now.

If you use AIDA in everything it will become a habit. A good habit. So call me now and tell me you have reached this page in the book and what you think so far. ***No, I MEAN it***. *I need your feedback.* My contact details are in the Author's foreword. Your letters, email marketing, website content, content marketing will all be better if they pass the AIDA test. Even signage on a vehicle needs a call to action. Phone Now!

If you are going to send marketing e mails, or letters, only send them out in batches of ten or fifteen. Send the first batch to the least important targets and measure the response. Move up your list so that when you reach the most important targets you have got your content to be the best it can be. Get help with this if you need it. You do not want to burn the whole list learning how to get it right.

Another glaring mistake that people make when writing copy is who they focus on. You have to write things from the reader's viewpoint. Focus on the word *"you"*. "If *you* engage with us *you* will get, *you* will experience. This reads quite differently from "*we* do this really well". Using a phrase like 'our customers say' with some testimonials has much more power than 'We are really good at' whatever you do. Put yourself in the customers (or reader's) shoes. Framing it this way shows them you care and that you are a market-led business.

Branding

This area is one where you need professional help. Your brand is not just a logo. It is the entire image you create for the business. It is a tone that is created by your choices whether it is colours, typeface signs on a vehicle and even backgrounds. It carries through your website and all your communications. A good designer will even suggest that the typeface (font) on your computer (which you can change to suit) will match the one on your web page, business card and so on. Your brand is a small but significant element of how you influence your target customer to buy from you. Look at an accountant or a solicitor's web page and a food or clothing retailer. You will see the difference. Even the name of your business is part of your brand because as we mentioned in the internet section it has to be easy for google to find.

Content Marketing

Note that much of the information in this section is about indirect marketing. Many of the marketing experts today talk about content marketing. The definition: Content marketing is a strategic marketing approach focused on creating and distributing valuable, relevant and consistent information to attract and retain a clearly defined audience — and, ultimately, to drive profitable customer action. It is a very slow process but plant enough of it… More simply, content marketing is providing something for free in order to get the customer to engage so that you can sell them on the overall product. This is ideal for businesses where you have to educate your target customer as to why they should buy any product at all and specifically buy from you.

What, of what you know, can you afford to give away in order to sell more of it? The idea of you as a subject matter expert, which I already mentioned fits this model very well.

There are many things that impact your credibility in the eyes of the customer. The biggest of these is customer service. It seems obvious but not to everyone. You have already created a customer relationship policy through your response to the eight P's. So that when an issue arises you know what to do without having to think about it first. To use jargon you have a policy and a procedure to be followed for most of the business processes.

Here is a quick comparison just for clarity:

Direct	Indirect
• In-person sales calls • Print or media advertising • Telephone sales calls • Email advertise- ment campaigns • Direct mail, flyer or sales letters • Promoted or paid advertis- ing on social media • Pre-roll ads on YouTube and other video platforms	• Search Engine Optimization • News articles and press • Sponsorships • Useful blog posts • Social media fan pages • Social media influencers • Product placements • Referrals • Online reviews

I have avoided much of the advertising options because I am not a fan of blanket advertising. I feel that in general they fit into the spray and pray category. I want for a moment, however, to revert to the **case study** I used earlier.

The beautician working in Dublin 17 starts by thinking it is all women from 17 to 70 but quickly recognises that 80% of her clients are 25–35 in age. When she looks a bit deeper she finds that most of them are employed in clerical roles in Dublin city centre. Now she has them geographically, by age, by gender and by spending power. She can pitch her price to suit what they can spend weekly or monthly. Knowledge is power. It also means that she can write her marketing material to speak specifically to her target. After all what attracts a 25–35 year old is very different from the message you send to a 55+ customer. This is as direct as you can be when advertising. You make the offer to your actual ideal client and exclude the rest. Best of all you can measure the results.

If your business is B2C it is common sense for you to segment your target market like she did. Sending one message to the younger women after work and an entirely different message, at 10 a.m., to the ladies-who-lunch. If you break it down (segment it) you can offer completely different services to the different ages who are at different stages in life.

You can usefully advertise a clear message to a market that is segmented in this way. Segmenting the market is like going fishing for salmon. You can of course put out a big net and fill it. But then you have to sort through all the fish you don't want to find that you have only six salmon in the net. You will probably catch more salmon faster with a fishing rod, the right bait and a lot less effort.

I mentioned earlier too that most businesses get 80% of the revenue from 20% of the customers so why do we pursue the rest of the fish in the net when the profitable 20%, the salmon, is where we should be focused.

This leads me to just remind you that the best marketing you can do, once you have a customer base is to look after those customers. They call that Customer Relationship

Management (CRM). It costs a lot of money to get a new client. It only makes sense to invest a few Euro in retaining them. What will you do?

I'll sum up the marketing section of the chapter with another nice definition of marketing:

Good marketing is sending a specific message to a target audience to inform them how you meet their already expressed need.

Sales is different.

Sales is the activity we do to convert the marketing awareness into money. Every business is in sales. Every business owner is a seller. You cannot afford to be passive about selling. A big mistake would be NOT to get out out and hustle because the business will run out of customers, and therefore out of money, and ultimately fail. So this page in this book could be the point where you re-focus. The most important person in any business is the salesperson. The best sales people should be paid the highest salaries because they create the work for everyone else in the business to do.

I read somewhere that most sales of larger ticket items come after a minimum of six contacts. Most sales people give up after three or four. So persistence (without pestering) is one of the key qualities of a sales person. It doesn't have to be pushy at all. In fact the best definition of sales I heard was 'Sales is the facilitation of the customer through the buying process'. The seller knows the route and acts like a harbour pilot, helping the buyer to avoid all the rocks and obstacles on the way to a mutually beneficial destination. Ethical selling says you don't sell something to someone unless they actually want or need it and can afford to pay for it.

The most important sales skill is *closing*. To do that there are two key sub skills: Overcoming objections and asking for the order.

An **objection** is the fear a buyer has around the purchase. Asking questions around those objections is the best tool to overcome them. Most good sales people try to get a series of yes answers, a series of agreements to minor points before the final request for the order. For example: You like the colour? Yes. And you are okay on the delivery date? Yes. (These are temperature checking questions.) Now we go for the close: Let's go and sign the agreement. NO. This is good because you can now ask: Oh right so what is between us and a deal? They tell you and you ask: If I can fix that then we have a deal? Yes. You outline how you sort things out and ask for the order again. Don't wait for the customer to buy. Ask for the sale.

The ultimate sales and marketing book for me is the Joe Girard book I already mentioned. I can't do justice to the topic in four paragraphs. However what I will say is that if you are not willing to be a very active seller and marketer then you probably should close this book now and go and do something more productive instead. If you don't want to sell then this is the wrong route for you. People buy from people and right now you are the people in your business. There is no avoiding it. *The reason many small businesses fail is lack of sales*. The reason for the lack of sales is that nobody knows about the business. Without marketing and sales then there is no business.

Simply think of it. This book is a sales tool for my business. If you got anything at all from the book, can you imagine how much more you would get if you work with me, one-to-one, to help build your business? You and I both have to sell. Every day.

One of the most effective tools in this toolbox is making it easy for the customer to pay you. Card? Electronic Fund Transfer? Cash? Staged Payments? Finance? Discuss this with your customer as part of closing the sale and there will be no nasty surprises for you or for them. Remember a sale is a contract for you to provide and for them to pay. It only works if we all win.

Checklist

ACTION	☑
Identify your ideal customer	☐
Define the marketing channel (how they get to know about you and your business)	☐
Write the copy, using **AIDA**, to attract them	☐
Implement the strategy, on a test and measure basis, reaching small groups to start	☐
Close the sales	☐
Do it again	☐
Ask for referrals and testimonials	☐
Keep marketing	☐
Find additional targets and repeat the process	☐

Part Three

Fire

Fire

Finance and Tax

The Finance section invites you to get to grips with your own relationship with money. Is it a motivator for you? How do you feel about asking a customer to pay you? And quite simply where will you get the money you need to finance the business.

The advisors you choose can move you forward or hold you back so choosing an accountant, a solicitor or a bank or a mentor can be critical.

In regard to Tax: It is a fact of life so there is basic information on most of what you will meet and more details where it is more likely you have to deal with it.

Insurance & Employment
Insurance is really just a decision on which provider. Again you need the right adviser.

Employing people is the most heavily regulated area of business. I have attempted to put the key information from recruitment to dismissal and all points in between and there is a lot of it.

Regulation
We operate in a very regulated business world and you need to be sure that there is not a requirement on you to

be registered with a regulatory body. Make sure you have ticked that box.

Engage is the final word and It speaks for itself.

The most dangerous pothole in the whole road to starting a business could be health and safety so again make sure that you get that done.

The last duck you need to get in a row before you start is the rainy day fund. Lots of people leave it to year two. I would prefer that you at least consider it now.

The final chapter is really just a last check to be sure you haven't left anything important behind. It's like checking for your passport on the way to the airport. Sometimes you wish you had done it before you left the house.

Chapter 9:
Finance and Taxation

Finance means money and if the truth is stated that is what it is all about. Without the money why bother. Without the money it is just a hobby. That is why you have to have a strategy to get paid as discussed earlier. As with just about every topic there are books about this too and I have to choose what to include as a start-up book. For me there are four things we have to deal with in this chapter.

1. Funding the business
2. Choosing a Bank
3. Choosing an Accountant and a Solicitor
4. Your relationship with the taxman across all the taxes you might have to pay

1. Funding the Business
Funding is all about how you manage the financial risk. Lenders are much more inclined to support things with a low financial risk profile. They don't want to be alone – which means you have to carry your share of the risk (usually a minimum of 20% of the set-up costs). You can often satisfy this by investing personal assets – your car, your computer, your tools, etc. You also need to demonstrate your ability to repay. If you are funding the business solely from your savings you might have another look at SURE *(page 43)*.

The quick list of potential funding sources:
- Angel investors
- Banks
- Credit Union
- Crowd funding (Linked Finance, Grid Finance, Fundit, Kickstarter, Spark)
- Microfinance Ireland *(page 14)*
- Rich Relatives
- Strategic Banking Corporation of Ireland – via Bank of Ireland or Ulster Bank *(page 45)*
- The Employment and Investment Incentive Scheme *(page 44)*
- Your own resources.

These are all relevant to some people and some are relevant to all. Most have been covered in the support chapter. The big question is how much do you need to get the business to a point of viability? I mentioned risk earlier. Business is a calculated risk. If you did the business plan you have already done the calculations. If not this would be a perfect time to do them.

2. Choosing a bank

The bank you choose has a real impact on the growth of your business. Most will offer free fees for the first two years of a new business. Almost all offer a business credit card service. This type of card gives you a really good corroborative record for your spend each month. You never get

> **Nugget:**
> *Banks are there to serve you. Not the other way around. Be prepared to change banks to get what you need*

charged interest because the card is cleared every month by direct debit. You do of course have to have the cash in your account to clear it. If the bank won't offer the card I would call that a deal-breaker.

To open an account you need proof of identity and your certificates from CRO. I suggest having 3 accounts. A normal current account to use for your day to day transactions, a savings account for the income tax and VAT money (which isn't yours anyway) and a 30 day notice account for your rainy day fund.

Overdraft facilities are really valuable. They allow you to pay bills while you are waiting to be paid by a client. They are not intended to be used all the time just occasionally. Lots of business owners don't get that. You will need a clean credit report to be granted an overdraft or a credit card facility. Go to *https://www.centralcreditregister.ie/* and apply for your report. Sometimes they have got it wrong and you can get it fixed. Sometimes what you thought was holding you back isn't there any more. Knowledge is power and the information is free.

Really you have four options in the Irish Market:

- AIB
- Bank of Ireland
- KBC
- Ulster Bank

These are looking for commercial business.

Go and meet the people at the bank you choose. Pick the one where you can have a long term relationship with the people not the institution. Make sure they will offer you the help you need. If you find that it is difficult to do business with your bank then tell them, and if nothing changes go somewhere else.

3. Choosing the accountant

The accountant you pick should be someone who comes recommended. They should also be firmly in your corner, doing their best to minimise the amount of tax you are paying. They should be advising you on what the accounts are telling you about the health of your business. I always expect the accountant to find his fee in the money he saves me over the year by virtue of smart tax planning or cost management or a combination of both. Some accountants don't think like that and in my opinion they are not suited to working with small business. You should also negotiate a fixed price with the accountant before you re appoint them each year. The accountant should be pretty much cost neutral, finding their fee by helping you apply for and receive grants and by minimising the amount of taxes you and the business pay.

Choosing a solicitor

There will be situations like contracts for example where you will need the advice of a solicitor. Picking one at this stage makes a lot of sense. You are not under pressure and you have time to find the right person. The solicitor you use for business needs to be a business focused person; someone who has litigation experience. You may need that in the future. A person who specialises in conveyancing property or family law has a different skillset so choose carefully.

4. Your relationship with the taxman.

This is a whole of life relationship so it might as well be a pleasant one.

The taxes you are likely to encounter:

A. As a self-employed person or a business owner you must register for income tax, through the Revenue Online Service (ROS), as soon as you start to trade. Rates of personal tax are 20% and 40% in 2019 and are unchanged for 2020.

B. We mentioned Value added Tax (VAT). You don't have to register for this until your turnover (total sales value) in the calendar year exceeds €37,500 for a service business. It would be €75,000 if you supply goods. Rates are 9%, 13.5% and 23% depending on industry. There are several other special rates for specific industries but the're not relevant to most start-ups.

C. Employee PAYE. If you have employees you must register on ROS and deduct the tax, PRSI and USC in line with the document provided by Revenue. You must either allow Revenue to direct debit your account or make a payment by the 19th of each month.

D. If you are a limited company you must register for Corporation tax. The rate is 12.5%

E. If you sell something outside of normal trade and make a profit on it then you may be subject to Capital Gains Tax at 33% on that profit

F. Capital acquisitions tax (inheritance or gift tax) is chargeable at 33% on gifts over a value of €3,000 in any one year. There are a series of lifetime limits on inheritance depending on the relationship between you and the person leaving the inheritance.

Here are the key pieces of information in regard to each tax:

Income tax

The return document (form 11) is filled in on ROS. It is for the previous year. So for example in 2020 the return which must be submitted by October 31 of that year is in fact your formal declaration of what you owe for the tax year 2019. In 2019 you might or might not have paid preliminary tax. If you did it was based on your best estimate in October of your likely bill for 2019.

Each year in October you must pay 90% of what you think you owe for the current year (in our example 2020). This is preliminary tax. You must also pay the balance between what you paid as preliminary tax in 2019 and the actual total on the final form 11. If you paid no preliminary tax in 2019, because perhaps it was year-1 and you didn't think you owed anything, then you owe all the tax for 2019. This might just be a minimum PRSI payment of €500 PLUS the preliminary tax for 2020. The amount owed includes Income tax, PRSI and Universal Social Charge. That is why you should put money aside each month so it will not hurt too much.

ROS will do the tax calculations for you, on Form 11, once you input the numbers from your accounts. Revenue *will* accept preliminary tax paid monthly by direct debit.

VAT

This is a tax on the value you add to each product or service. You have to do the return online every two months and again make the payment by the 19th of the following month.

The simplest way to show how it works is by an example:

I had sales in the period of	€3,000 plus VAT
The VAT I must send to revenue is 23% of €3,000	€690
I can reduce this amount by reclaiming VAT I paid to my suppliers in the period which is commonly referred to as getting the VAT back. You don't usually get money it just reduces the amount you pay to revenue	€385
Total due to revenue	€305

There are some industries, like car mechanics and builders, where the VAT rate is reduced from 23% to 13.5%. Newspapers and some other things attract 9%. There are some industries like training where the VAT is zero or exempt. For most businesses however the rate is 23%. There is a list on Revenue where you can check the rate appropriate to your business and the web address is *https://revenue.ie/en/vat/vat-rates/search-vat-rates/index.aspx.* You must register and charge VAT once you are making sales of €37,500 or €3,125 every month. If registering make sure you tick the box to do so on a cash-received basis. Otherwise you will have to pay the VAT as soon as you send the invoice and it could be a month before you receive the money.

Once you are VAT registered you must do a VAT 3 (online) every two months.

The headings on a VAT 3 are:

T1 Vat on Sales	It is the VAT content of all money received
T2 Vat on purchases	All the VAT on your allowable receipts for the period
Subtract T2 from T1	
T3 Vat Payable	If (T1 minus T2) is a positive number that is the amount you send to Revenue and you enter it here
T4 Vat repayable	If T1 minus T2 is a negative number (if T2 is bigger than T1). This rarely happens but if it does you enter it here and it is the amount Revenue sends to you.

PAYE

(if you are a company director OR if you employ staff)

If you have employees you must make a monthly return to detail how much you paid them and how much you deducted on behalf of Revenue. If people are on the same amount each month Revenue suggests that it would be the same as last time. They direct debit that amount unless you tell them differently. You also must pay 10.75% Employers PRSI so paying someone 2,000 a month will cost a total of €2,215. The 10.75% is not payable for business owners who are company directors or sole traders.

Here is the worked up example, for one month, which is also what a payslip might look like based on the rates in force at the time of writing:

Salary (Paid Monthly)		€2,000
Income tax @20%	€400	
Less tax credit	€250	
Tax due		€150
PRSI @ 4%		€80
Universal Social Charge	€1.001 @ 0.5% €655 @ 2.0% €344 @ 4.5%	€5.01 €13.10 €15.48
Total deductions		€264.59
Net Pay		**€1,735.41**
Employers PRSI	10.75%	€215.00
Total due to Revenue this month		€479.59
Total cost of having the employee €2,215 per month		

In 2020 there will be an additional €12.50 net pay per month because the tax credit increases to €262.50.

Relevant Contracts Tax (RCT)

This is a retention tax operated in construction, forestry meat processing and some haulage.

The main contractor and the sub-contractor must be registered for RCT with Revenue. Again an example is easiest:

Sub-contractor bids €1,000 for the work. Main contractor contacts revenue and is told to retain 20% or 35% and send it to revenue. So the sub-contractor receives the 80% or the 65% and a cert to say that the rest was sent to revenue. He may then apply to have the tax repaid and may be granted that depending on his tax status. If a sub-contractor applies to Revenue and is granted a C2 card then no RCT is charged. A C2 is rarely issued to Year-1 businesses. If the main contractor fails to deduct RCT *HE* is liable to pay the 20% or 35%. They are very sticky on this.

Professional Services Witholding Tax (PSWT)

This is similar to RCT. If you are a professional in any of the following fields: Medical, Architectural, Engineering, Accountant, Legal, Financial, Economic, Marketing, Advertising, Business and you do work for a semi-state or government body they will first require a tax clearance access number. Then they must withold 20% and give you the relevant cert (F45). Again you can apply for repayment or to have the tax offset.

Corporation tax

This is income tax for companies paid at 12.5% on Net Profit. It has to be paid 8 months after the year end. If you own the company your personal tax must be on PAYE but you don't have to pay the Employers PRSI.

Capital Gains Tax

This is unlikely to be an issue but let's say you have a machine you bought for €5,000. You used it for 2 years, adapted it and then decided to replace it with a better one. Because you adapted it You can sell it for €9,000 This is a capital gain of €4,000 and is subject to CGT at 33%. There is no CGT on the first €1,250 in each tax year so the tax of 33% is not on the €4,000 but on €2,750 making €907.50.

Inheritance Tax

- In your lifetime you can inherit €320,000 from your parents, combined – €335,000 from 2020 on. After the limit it is subject to 33%

- You can inherit €32,500 from a grandparent or sibling
- Everyone else is €16,250. You can receive €3,000 in any one year from anyone you like without impacting these limits or paying any capital Acquisitions Tax

I can't stress enough that if you do everything that you should, and on time, then you will have no problem with Revenue.

If you fall behind at any point *talk to them*. They will do everything they can to help you to get back on track.

If you are in business you should have a tax clearance cert. That will allow you to pitch for work in the state sector or even for community groups that have funding. It is a five minute job – online, of course.

Nugget:

Ignoring Revenue is the kind of mistake that can have huge consequences, personally and financially.

Finance and Taxation Checklist

ACTION	☑
Work up the numbers on the set-up costs and add 10% for the unforeseen	☐
Research the bank, accountant and meet the people	☐
Open the bank accounts, appoint the accountant / solicitor	☐
Decide how much the accountant will do for you and negotiate a fixed price	☐
Secure the funding you require. Don't be tempted to start without the funding.	☐
Get your ROS set up (it can take 10 days) but only register on the day you start trading	☐
Get your tax clearance cert once registered	☐

Chapter 10:
Insurance & Employing People

Insurance

Insurance is one of those things that you don't spend time thinking about. It's a Just Do IT moment.

Pick a good broker. Make sure they are not just an insurance agent because they are tied to the products of just one company. Ensure that they have authorised advisor status from the Central Bank. If they don't have that go elsewhere. What the rules for an authorised advisor say is that even if you don't put the business through them they are legally obliged to give you the best advice possible. In the event of a claim the brokers know how to handle things. They have the relevant experience. Using a broker allows you to continue running your business while they deal with the problems. They don't usually charge for claims work.

You should have Public Liability, and either Product Liability or Professional Indemnity. If you don't buy insurance, and something goes wrong, then you could find yourself personally liable, paying a claim for the rest of your life.

If you have staff you MUST have Employers Liability. Most business policies cover your office in the same way that your home insurance covers your home. It also covers,

Public Liability, Employers Liability and Professional Indemnity all in one. I suggest you do the instalment arrangement to manage cash flow better.

As I mentioned briefly earlier, *(page 23)*: if you use your own car for the business then you need to amend the insurance to cover 'use in association with the insured's business'. This is commonly known as a class 2 policy. Your basic car insurance only covers you for social, domestic and pleasure purposes and specifically excludes use for the business so don't long finger this.

The last insurances I want to mention are the ones which pay out if you have an accident or a specific illness. The premium is set based on the risks, so someone, mostly office based, is a lower risk than someone on a building site. A younger person is usually lower risk than someone older. The premium will reflect that. Because all of this can be complex you do need the specialist advice. This is the broker's expertise.

Employing People
Employing people is the most difficult part of owning a business.

If you decide to employ people consider your family first. Consider too that €100 a week subsidy from Jobstart if you employ a person on the dole.

If you do decide to employ someone (other than family), even part time, you are the subject of a pile of legislation. Most of the information you want is at this link. *https://www.workplacerelations.ie/en/publications_forms/guide_to_employment_rights_nera_.pdf*

This is provided by NERA. National Employment Rights Authority through the Workplace Relations Commission (WRC).

A quick summary of what you must have in place:

(a) A registration with Revenue as an employer and all employees registered.
(b) A contract
(c) Minimum Wage
(d) A proper induction process
(e) Paid Holidays. 8 hrs per 100 worked is minimum
(f) Records of hours worked
(g) A health and safety policy
(h) A Bullying and harassment policy
(i) Training in manual handling for all staff
(j) Grievance policy
(k) Disciplinary / Dismissals Policy
> *You must comply with minimum notice legislation if letting someone go; or pay them in lieu of notice*
(l) Parental Leave Policy
(m) You must provide
  i) Payslips (see example on page 119)
  ii) Rest breaks (with a place for staff to go away from their workstation)
  iii) Reasonable response to Force Majeure events (death, accident, illness of family or the employee)
(n) You must do at least annual performance reviews and provide feedback and a way for staff to raise issues that might arise

(o) You must provide access to a pension provider and be willing to deduct pension contributions from wages, and send them to the provider

(p) You must comply with GDPR in relation to personnel files including unsuccessful applicants for a job

(q) You must keep records of all of this and keep them up to date

It is a long list but there are template documents on line for all the policies. Go to *https://www.besmart.ie/* and build your safety statement for free.

I think having nobody in a role is better than having the wrong person. The wrong person eats your time because they are the wrong person or the wrong fit and that does your business more harm than good. I am just going to look at **the first hire** because in many ways the later ones are less critical. The first hire doubles the team and needs to bring an ability to fulfil multiple roles. Each one hired after that can be much more role specific.

The recruitment process starts with figuring out the weaknesses in your team. There is no point in adding another person just like you. That actually means you increase the weaknesses rather than stopping them. You need to employ someone whose strengths and character complements your own strengths. Ideally a person who will excel at and enjoy doing all the things you hate to do. If you are a big picture visionary person then you need someone who is detail focused, for example.

Writing a job description

The first step is to list all the tasks you want carried out. Write the list. Ask yourself 'is it possible for one person to do what you want'. I promise that it will shorten the process and help you get the right person first time.

Second; **write a person description.** What kind of person are they? While you cannot discriminate in your choice on any of the nine equality grounds, you need to know who you are looking for. Write it down in terms of skill, knowledge, qualifications, experience and any intangibles like connections in the industry.

(*https://www.citizensinformation.ie/en/employment/equality-in-work/equality-in-the-workplace.html*)

Advertising the role

You can advertise and recruit directly or you can pay a recruiter up to 20% of the annual salary to do it for you. Both have advantages and disadvantages.

https://www.irishjobs.ie/ is a free national forum to advertise jobs. It is linked to DEASP so you get applications from unemployed people who might qualify for Jobstart funding. There is another agency SEETEC (*https://www.seetec.ie/*) who also work with unemployed people and will find local candidates for you for free. In the advert require that they tell you in the letter of application why they are a good fit for the job. If they fail to do that (and loads do) then you really don't want them because they can't follow simple instructions. Make the job description and person specification available to help candidates to know what you want.

Shortlisting

You only want to interview real candidates, ones who can follow instructions and fit the role. One applicant usually stands out in a bunch in my experience. So read the letters of application and see who fits before you look at the CV. Only interview a maximum of 5 people for no more than 30 minutes each.

The interview process

Next you need to create a score sheet and a set of questions. You need to ask each candidate the same list of questions and score people on their responses. Add additional questions but make sure to ask them all the questions on the list. Have at least 2 people on the panel so that you can compare impressions. Now you have an impartial evaluation of the candidate. It also allows that if the unsuccessful person asks why they didn't get the job you can show that the winner scored higher on whatever area they fell down on. If you don't get the right candidate: don't hire. Advertise again in a different forum.

Do the decent thing. Communicate with everyone whether or not you are going to hire them tell them they weren't shortlisted or came third at interview.

Every new hire is on probation for 6 months. I received an amazing piece of advice which still rattles in my head sometimes 'if it is not working out be prepared to fire them early on and move on'. Sometimes the one who scored second best is the right hire. It's a bit like a talent show. Often the second place competitor goes on to a better career than the winner.

On the other hand, you must remember that the person can take up to six months before they reach full productivity. They have to learn your way of doing things, become familiar with their responsibilities. Don't make excuses for someone who doesn't fit but do, as in all other areas of the business, test and measure. It will cost money until they are up to speed. I regret that but it is true. Be prepared to absorb that cost. It will hurt the bottom line at first but after 6 months they should be at least cost neutral and hopefully they will be a net contributor to the bottom line.

A great many business owners don't gain full value from their team because they micro manage them. This demotivates the employee and wastes the employer's time. My choice would be what is called management by objective. You tell the employee what is expected and when. You can then measure the quality and timeliness of the work at a single point. If that isn't comfortable build in some milestones. Don't insist they do it your way. They should of course follow the system but leave them some room for putting their own stamp on things. They might innovate some new faster cheaper better way to do something. If not they have your way to fall back into.

There is a point in many businesses where a big mistake is made. Sometimes the person themselves becomes more important than the role they fulfil in the business. You cannot let that happen. The health of the business is the most important thing. If letting one person go maintains or improves that health then don't delay, do it. It is hard but very necessary. When a role is no longer viable (redundant) then find something else for the person to do or let them go.

Insurance & Employment Checklist

ACTION	☑
Appoint an insurance broker, making sure they are an authorised advisor	☐
Take their advice on the appropriate cover and levels of cover for your business	☐
Change motor cover to class 2	☐
If employing: • Create the safety statement • Put all the policies etc. in place *before* starting to recruit • Do job description • Create person specification • Make both of these available to candidates • Choose a way to advertise the role • Interview • Respond to everyone	☐

Chapter 11:
Regulation

First you need to decide on a structure for your business.

- **Sole trader.** (which is just you)
- **Partnership.** You and any number of others in a structure with one bank account
- **Ltd Company**. You alone or with others operating a separate legal entity where your liability for any loss is limited to the value of your investment in the company

If you are going into business with others then you are not obliged to but you should create a partnership or shareholders agreement. If you do that, everyone's role is clear and there is an exit route if one person wants to leave.

No matter what structure you use there are mandatory registrations. There are also industry specific registrations. What follows is a broad spectrum for start-ups.

Sole Trader:
Business name: If you are using a name other than your own you must register a business name with the Companies Registration Office (CRO) it costs €20 online €40 paper. You won't be able to open the business bank account with your business name without the cert from this.

Income Tax:
You must register for Income Tax on a self-assessment basis. You do this by creating an identity on either Ros (Revenue online service) or myGovID (*https://www.mygovid.ie/*) and selecting register as a self-employed person. Partnerships must register both as an entity and as individuals.

Each year you must do a tax return (via ROS) before 31st October or pay a surcharge on your taxes.

PAYE, VAT and RCT: These are done in exactly the same way on ROS. Only do these if you must.

Partnerships must do exactly the same.

Ltd Companies must first be created using the CRO. Some people pay for this service (between €100 and €300) but it is possible to do it yourself.

A Company must submit a corporation tax return to Revenue It must also submit an annual return every year to CRO. Companies turning over less than €4 million can avail of easier CRO returns processes. Failure to make a return by the due date means you must submit audited accounts each of the next 3 years. An audit costs €2–4,000 each year.

General Data Protection Regulations (GDPR)
This came into force in May 2018. If you hold data on a person or a company that is not publicly available then you are subject to GDPR. Some basic information:

1. You must check if you should be registered with the data protection commissioner
2. You must protect the personal data you hold

3. You must have a valid reason to hold it
   Ideally, written permission which includes the reason and duration for keeping the data
4. You must either get permission to hold the data or delete it
5. You must delete data within 30 days if requested to do so
6. You must nominate a person to be responsible
7. You must write a policy for managing data

If point one is a 'No' then you should just use common sense and keep information to yourself. The most important thing is to not hold and especially not share other people's personal data without their permission.

In lots of industries there is specific regulation:

- If you deal with children on vulnerable adults you probably need Garda vetting
- If you are in Food then you must register with the Health Service Executive (HSE) and have your kitchen approved by a health inspector and you must be trained in HACCP (Hazard and Critical Control Points)
- In the security industry it is the Private Security Authority
- An electrician needs RECI (Register of Electrical Contactors)
- Most Plumbers need to be Registered Gas Installers (RGI) certainly this is needed in the cities or you miss a lot of business
- Taxis are under the control of the TaxI Regulator.
- Accountants are usually members of professional

associations
- Driving instructors and professional truck or bus drivers are the Road Safety Authority
- Architects cannot call themselves architects without permission from the Royal Institute of Architects in Ireland
- Estate agents must be registered with the Property Services Regulatory Authority
- Nursing Homes are under the Supervision of HIQA (Health Information and Quality Authority)
- Anything to do with Finance or Insurance is the Central Bank

In total there are over 200 bodies so check if you are subject to regulation as part of your research. If you are, there will be a fee so build that into your set up costs.

Health and Safety

This is a topic where it is possible to get a degree so I hope to raise your awareness and get you to dig deeper yourself rather than attempt to be comprehensive. The whole sphere is overseen by the Health and Safety Authority. (HSA) Much of the training is overseen by Solas especially in relation to construction and quarrying. The Safepass is the minimum certification to enter a building site along with suitable PPE (personal protection equipment).

An employer has a legal obligation to protect workers from injury under health and safety legislation. You need the safety statement, manual handling training, perhaps fire safety and first aid depending on individual circumstances. What dictates all of this is the risk assessment carried out as part of the safety statement. You can develop your safety statement for free and learn most of what you need on *https://www.besmart.ie/* Doing the process makes you not just safety aware but safety conscious. Carry out the risk assessments honestly and minimise the risk to yourself and others including members of the public and you are probably compliant. I think you should do it now, while you have time, before you get too busy and end up putting it on the long finger. Mostly it is common sense. Keep people away from danger. If they must be at risk make sure the risk is as low as possible. If you fail to do that, even limited liability will not necessarily protect you as company directors can be held personally responsible under the act. Don't avoid this one.

Rainy Days
This is a subject close to my heart. Living in Ireland, it rains a lot. I am sure you understand. However in business you need one simple word in this regard. *Provide*.

When things go wrong it is too late to start thinking about this. My suggestion is simple. Over the first three years build up a squirrel-like reserve. Put aside enough money to give your business enough to carry you through 6 months with no revenue at all.

What that does for you is it allows you to take advantage of opportunities that arise. It means you don't have to go to the bank looking for a loan to capitalise growth. If things go bad, you get ill or have an accident, there is money to cover you. Perhaps it could pay to bring someone in to keep things going while you recover. It is there to to facilitate a change of direction in the business in response to a downturn. If that's not there then you are in trouble. You have no buffer and it could kill your business.

Salt away 6 months money. Put it in a bank account in your business bank but make that account an account where you have to give 30 days' notice of your intent to withdraw money. You can also use this as security against a loan or an overdraft and so the business can go on.

Smart business owners provide for rainy days.

Checklist

ACTION	☑
Choose the structure that suits you	☐
Register what you need to	☐
Check the regulatory environment and fulfil any obligations	☐
Check your GDPR situation	☐
Deal with the health and safety stuff now	☐
Create your rainy day provision	☐

Chapter 12:
Engage

We have reached the final chapter. All there is left to do now is review all your action lists, make sure that:

- the research is done
- the marketing is ready
- the first sale is lined up
- and the tax registration is in place

…and you are ready for your first day as a self-employed person.

This is the moment when your life changes, when you change to become the business owner you dreamt of being. You have made it real, or you haven't. If you have things to do yet, take careful note of what you haven't done. This is like a sales pitch. These are your last few objections, the last few barriers between the old you and the new.

This is the point in any episode of Star Trek the Next Generation (forgive me this) where everything is done, the course set, the speed determined all that is required is that one word to make it a reality: *Engage*.

There is no substitute for action and all through this book if you have been completing the checklists then there is nothing between you and your new business.

To close, I'd like to sum up what I think about us: Me, the writer, and you, the reader.

If you Google the word Enterprise the first thing to come up is Star Trek. But to us, we're small business owners not some kind of space cadets. We have started a business so what we are, is Entrepreneurs. Enterprising People.

When you look Enterprise up in the dictionary it implies that enterprising people are Calculated RISK TAKERS. Go a little further and it implies that we are *Industrious, Hardworking People* and that an enterprise is a systematic activity directed toward profit.

This is not a bad definition against which to measure yourself.

Calculated Risk:

Every business decision is a calculated risk – or is it? Sometimes we take a punt, go on instinct. Since instinct is often good among entrepreneurs at least half the time we get it right. Ask yourself: If I took time to 'calculate the risk', to look at the situation or opportunity and work out the detail, would I behave differently? In order to make the most of the opportunity that now presents itself you need to look honestly at your attitude to risk. Are you eager for, indifferent to or averse to risk? Are you a hare or a tortoise; quick or slow approach? No wrong answers here just improved awareness.

Industrious, Hard Workers.

It is harder than it used to be to get work. It's not impossible. Working harder won't necessarily get you the result you want but listening to what customers want and meeting that need will, and that's working smart. There is an old saying the harder I work the luckier I get. Hard work and a willingness to do it will always give a positive result. Smart work seeks opportunity, goes out and gets it, while others sit and complain about there being no work. Both together, in the right proportions get great results.

A Systematic Activity Directed Toward Profit.

To develop a systematic approach we have again to look at what we do under a few headings and then ask ourselves some questions about what we are doing. In this we must always remember if it is not broken don't fix it, just repeat it. Often.

What do we do really well? What business just comes in every week or month?	• Who buys it? • Why do they choose us? • How can I add value to those customers? • What else do they buy? • Can I provide that at a profit? • AND what else do they NEED?

The answers to these questions lead you to knowing your unique selling proposition. When you know that you can offer it to others as well as your current clients and so grow your business. Now you have a TARGET and a METHOD of reaching that target. All that is left is the Action to go and empower your own success.

The Bottom Line:

All we have to do is remember our continuing mission; to seek out new products, new customers and go boldly after business where we haven't gone before.

Final Checklist

ACTION	☑
Go back over all the other checklists and review them	☐
Take action on anything not yet done	☐
Review the milestones you created Have you hit them? On time?	☐
Delay starting if needs be to cover all bases	☐
Have you got the first sale lined up	☐
You only really start your business the day you sign the first contract or get the first payment. Have you done it?	☐
ENGAGE	☐

List of directory sites

This is a sample list and it is not exhaustive

https://www.adverts.ie/

http://www.bigdirectory.ie/

http://www.browse.ie/

http://www.citylocal.ie/

https://www.cylex.ie/

https://www.dublinbynumbers.com/

https://www.finditireland.com

https://www.goldenpages.ie/

https://www.hotfrog.ie/

https://www.infobel.com

https://www.irelandlookup.com/

http://www.irelands-directory.com/

https://www.irelandyp.com/

https://ie.kompass.com/

http://www.localsearch.ie/

https://www.localdirectory.ie/

http://mylocaltown.info/

https://www.mytown.ie/

https://www.onlinedirectories.ie/

https://www.ratemyarea.com/

https://redbook.ie/

http://www.search.ie/

https://www.startpage.com/

http://tradefinder.ie/

http://tradesmen.ie/

http://trustedtrades.ie/

https://www.tuugo.info

https://whatswhat.ie/

https://www.yabsta.ie/

https://www.yalwa.ie/

https://www.yelp.ie

https://www.yourlocal.ie/

https://www.yoys.ie/ (b2b)

Useful links

https://www.besmart.ie/

https://www.centralcreditregister.ie/

https://www.cro.ie/

https://khoros.com/resources/social-media-demographics-guidesocial-media-demographics-current

https://microfinanceireland.ie/

https://www.mygovid.ie/

https://platodublin.ie

https://www.psai.ie/

https://revenue.ie

https://www.riai.ie/

https://www.ros.ie

https://safeelectric.ie/

https://sbci.gov.ie/

https://sbci.gov.ie/schemes/sme-credit-guarantee-scheme-cgs

http://www.welfare.ie

https://www.irishjobs.ie/

https://www.localenterprise.ie/

https://www.mabs.ie/en/how_we_help/debt_and_budgeting_tools/mabs_budgeting.html

https://revenue.ie/en/employing-people/employee-expenses/travel-and-subsistence/civil-service-rates.aspx

https://www.seetec.ie/

https://www.workplacerelations.ie/en/publications_forms/guide_to_employment_rights_nera_.pdf

https://revenue.ie/en/vat/vat-rates/search-vat-rates/index.aspx

Jargon buster

AIDA	Attention, Interest, Desire, Action
BTWEA	Back to Work Enterprise Allowance
CAO	Central Applications office
CAT	Capital Acquisitions Tax (Inheritances and Gifts)
CGT	Capital Gains Tax
CPC	Certificate of Professional Competence
CRM	Customer Relationship Management
CRO	Companies Registration office
CV	Curriculum Vitae
DEASP	Department of Employment Affairs and Social Protection
EI	Enterprise Ireland
EII	Employment and Investment Incentive
EL	Employers Liability (Insurance)
ESG	Enterprise Support Grant
GDPR	General Data Protection Regulations
HACCP	Hazard and Critical Control Points
HIQA	Health Information and Quality Authority
HSA	Health and Safety Authority
HSE	Health Service Executive
NERA	National Employment Rights Authority
PI	Professional Indemnity (Insurance)
PL	Public Liability (Insurance)
PPC	Pay Per Click
PPE	Personal Protection Equipment

PRSI	Pay Related Social Insurance
PSAI	Private Security Authority of Ireland
PSWT	Professional Services Withholding Tax
QQI	Quality Qualifications Ireland
RCT	Relevant Contracts Tax
RECI	Register of Electrical Contractors of Ireland
RIAI	Royal Institute of Architects Ireland
STEA	Short Term Enterprise Allowance
SURE	Start-Up Relief for Entrepreneurs
SWOT	Strengths Weaknesses, Opportunities, Threats
SYOB	Start Your Own Business
USC	Universal Social Charge
USED	Utilise, Stop, Exploit, Defend
VAT	Value Added Tax
WRC	Workplace Relations Commission